Success and the Fear of Success in Women

David W. Krueger, M.D.

THE FREE PRESS
A Division of Macmillan, Inc.
NEW YORK

Collier Macmillan Publishers
LONDON

The Free Press
A Division of Macmillan, Inc.
866 Third Avenue, New York, N.Y. 10022

Collier Macmillan Canada, Inc.

Printed in the United States of America

printing number

1 2 3 4 5 6 7 8 9 10

Library of Congress Cataloging in Publication Data

Krueger, David W.
  Success and the fear of success in women.

  Bibliography: p.
  Includes index.
  1. Fear of success. 2. Women—Mental health.
I. Title. [DNLM: 1. Achievement. 2. Women—Psychology.
BF 637.S8 K94a]
RC552. F43K78 1984   158.1'088042   83-48706
ISBN 0-02-918040-6

To two outstanding and successful women:
my wife and my daughter

Contents

Acknowledgments

———

I WOULD LIKE to acknowledge the women whose very hard work in therapy and in analysis has helped both themselves and me to better understand the issues discussed here. I am grateful to my former patients who agreed to review, edit, and allow publication of vignettes from their treatment. Their help in reviewing the material so that it is sufficiently disguised to protect anonymity yet substantially accurate is greatly appreciated.

Special thanks goes to two people: Bruce Richmond, who has provided invaluable help in editing both this and my previous work, and Debbie Silverman, my secretary, who has become painstakingly familiar with each word that will follow.

I am also very grateful for the collaboration with Dr. Carol Stark and Kitty Moore in the preparation of this manuscript; their suggestions were invaluable.

Introduction

WOMEN NOW HAVE ever-increasing social permission to participate fully in their own growth and realize their full human potential. Female autonomy and strength are culturally sanctioned,
and women need not live vicariously through men. Women have
discovered islands in themselves which have previously been disavowed, minimized, or disregarded. For some women, this process of discovery requires treatment to resolve issues and conflicts that are deeply buried in the strata of unconscious mental
processes. For others, without the deep bonds of unconscious
conflict, the awakening of society and of themselves has been
sufficient to launch them on a course of gratifying their inner-
most needs.

For some women, there are both external and internal factors
which inhibit achievement and successful, comfortable work in
whatever capacity chosen. With a decrease in the number of external impediments in recent years has come a better view of internal factors which inhibit growth. Now that so many new options are available, the predominant question becomes whether a
woman is able to exercise these options. If women no longer feel
restrained by parents, husbands, peers, or society, then the basic
issues shift from an external to an internal focus. The anatomy of

achievement is then organized around the functioning of intra-psychic components.

Achievement for women is not determined solely by discrimination or lack of opportunity, nor by their reversal. Deterrents to female achievement can emerge from developmental and intrapsychic elements, interwoven with socialization and its internalization.

The struggles which will be elaborated here are not difficulties arising primarily out of *current* societal discrimination or cultural oppression of women. The focus will be on *internal* obstacles to achievement and success, even in the presence of a facilitating environment. A study of unconscious intrapsychic conflict and its developmental history will illuminate some areas of the disallowal of success and/or success-striving. To love and to work in ways that are intimate and generative requires freedom from conventional stereotypes.

Adult women of today were not raised in the present cultural milieu. Their internal realities, conceptualizations, and fantasies, and their social and cultural behaviors, were formed largely in an earlier time. These early ideas and self-conceptualizations have a significant influence on women.

Until very recently, the cultural ego ideal for a successful woman included such character traits as submissiveness, dependency, and passivity. Such traits as assertiveness, independence, and ambition may currently be more adaptive, however. Because perceptions of the culturally ideal woman have changed, the traits once thought desirable may not benefit her as they did in the past. In fact, they may actually produce internal discomfort, and this disquietude may reach proportions which bring some women into treatment.

What has allowed some women to achieve their full potential to successfully consummate their goals while others succumb to pressure in avoidance of competitive achievement? This book is offered as a step in an evolving understanding of the many dynamic forces which impinge on the unique developmental process of the individual.

One perspective from which to examine the multidetermined issues of success and the impediments to success for women is the role of unconscious motivation. The substantive point of this book is the importance of developmental building blocks and unconscious motivation, and the ways in which they affect or determine conscious processes and events.

This book presents a multifactorial developmental and psychodynamic analysis of a pervasive symptom complex of the contemporary woman. The focus is on the conscious and unconscious mechanisms which a woman may employ to inhibit her own success. The scope of the book is an understanding of this symptom complex, the influences over developmental time, the various manifestations, and some therapeutic implications. Thus far, more work has been done in defining various inhibitions of achievement in men, with relative neglect of the unique developmental situations of women.

Success phobia is a specific and definite disturbance in the ability to comfortably complete or accept endeavors of achievement. One manifestation is work inhibition, a disturbance in functioning in a career in which one disallows successful completion of an endeavor, or sabotages or minimizes benefit or enjoyment when a task is brought to fruition.

The understanding and use of ego psychological principles, developmental data, and data from therapeutic and analytic experience requires differentiation and clear definition of the clinical picture in which a failure to achieve one's full potential predominates. This view of impediments to success is primarily an intrapsychic one, although it recognizes that many forces—biological, developmental, social, and environmental, among others—are components of the matrix which is incorporated and metabolized internally.

The work detailed here assumes relatively intact functioning of the person. The developmental deficits of schizophrenics and patients with more severe pathology beckon understanding of psychic structure at a different level; for these people an inhibition of success is only one piece in their puzzle of pathology.

To understand the psychodynamic constellation of a fear of success is, on the surface, a difficult matter. A fear of success—recoiling from that which one is constantly striving for and values—seems paradoxical. It may be difficult to comprehend the fear of achieving what has been long desired. Nonetheless, this fear is quite prevalent among contemporary women. Conflicts manifest themselves in social, career, or familial arenas to preclude opportunity, creativity, and achievement. As we witness more opportunity arising for women in roles formerly seen as the exclusive domain of men, there is also an unveiling of the issues which inhibit their striving.

The assumption weaving its way throughout most discourse on the subject of success is that it refers only to occupational or professional accomplishment. But this is not the case. Success for both men and women may find expression in the attainment of marriage and creative parenthood. Likewise, internal impediments to achievement can develop in many contexts and for varying reasons.

Until recently, the unavailability for some women of opportunities that involved responsibility and challenge meant they did not have to confront any inhibition about work or success since they have had little opportunity to come face to face with it. Alternate compensatory pathways for gratification were extolled, which precluded confrontation with the unconscious fantasies of what achievement would entail. Previous expectations of rejection may be replaced by the anxiety of competition now that competitive situations are accessible.

My observations on achievement and the different types of conflicts which preclude it have been based upon clinical experience with patients from many walks of life and many professions, including medicine, law, and business, as well as work within the home. My observations and earlier clinical studies, as well as those of other authors, focused on the psychodynamic origins of success phobia in men, largely because of the preponderance of clinical material from men. Because there are obvious similarities as well as divergences in the way men and women handle success and success phobia, an easy error in considering female psychology is the definition of female development in terms of male development or as a derivative of male experience.

In Freud's theory, femininity is revealed by the qualities of passivity, masochism, penis envy, a weak superego, and by the reproduction functions. Early views of female psychology, especially the psychoanalytic propositions of a deficient psychic structure, masochism, and a universal castration complex, are unsubstantiated by current psychoanalytic data. Psychoanalysis originally considered biological development as preeminent, eclipsing the role of culture or of purely psychological phenomena. This sense of female development was overgeneralized and was found ultimately to be clinically unsound. We now know a great deal more about early development, especially the first years of life. We have direct observations of normal infants and young children from which to draw data. In addition, there is a much greater appreciation of both pre- and post-Oedipal development, and we have more knowledge regarding the developmental psychology of the self.

Theory *informs* the listening position and guides both organization of data and understanding of observed processes. When theory *determines* listening, crucial issues may be overlooked.

Let us examine in greater detail what Kierkegaard adumbrated over a century and a half ago in talking of the anxiety of a successful endeavor: "The alarming possibility of being able causes dizziness."

I thought how unpleasant it is to be locked out; and I thought how it is worse perhaps to be locked in.

—Virginia Woolf
  A Room of One's Own

SECTION I

The Biological and Social Context for Achievement

CHAPTER 1

Biological and Social Variables: A Review and Reappraisal

A DIALOGUE WITH PATIENTS is a reflection of the dialogue of our times. Such a dialogue is never simple. Freud's work, viewed in the context of his times, made discoveries which were of his particular time and place. The universal principles which he discovered—the existence of the unconscious, psychic determinism, and the understandability of the human psyche—must be distinguished from derivations specific to that time and place, particularly in regard to the psychology of women. Freud elevated to clinical theory the provincial belief that the female regards herself as a "deficient man," and this concept has been recognized as an error with overwhelming and persistent clinical consequences.

Women now participate in many activities and endeavors which were once reserved for men. Sex-role stereotypes are gradually fading. Psychotherapists and psychoanalysts have been forced to reconsider the concepts of male and female development and personality.

The "traditional" woman for many generations limited her expansiveness to an acceptable "feminine" role entailing marriage, having children, and participating in domestic activities. She developed her own interests *within* this context. As the children gained autonomy and independence, her interests and work might have expanded outside the home. These women might otherwise have developed a strong sense of self, and their femininity and role as women may either have been essentially conflict-free or involved little compromise. These traditional women of the past may not have been neurotic and may have had no difficulty developing their full potential if the culture had been different. Traditional women are still hardly ever seen in treatment unless they experience a major life crisis, such as a failed marriage.

Boys do not have to compromise in this area. They are encouraged in their process of separation and autonomy by both parents and society, even to the point of celebrating their manhood with special ceremonies in many cultures. When young women try to become more autonomous, they often meet with the loss of family support. These young women may consider themselves "masculine" because of their pursuit of independence and may experience a combination of separation anxiety and anxiety about "going against the laws of nature."

Biological Variables

Much attention is paid to the physical differences between the sexes. Many women—and undoubtedly still more men—continue to believe that these physical differences outweigh any other differences. Although the debate still rages, I will not explore this important issue here. In an effort to examine the psychology of women in terms of achievement, it is important to note some basic biological differences in order to understand a woman's own sense of her developing self. What follows is a succinct discussion of information relevant to the biological differences between the sexes and their connection to a woman's self-definition.

For the first five to six weeks of life all embryos are morphologically female. At this time, sex genes assert and influence development. If the embryo is genetically male, germ cells at this time stimulate male hormones. Female development is autonomous; male development requires differentiation (1).

From birth on, there are biological and constitutional psychomotor differences between males and females. Females have greater motoric passivity at birth (2) and a greater sensitivity to pain and tactile stimuli than males (3). Females at age six months show a greater attention to auditory stimuli than do males, and have greater affective responses when seeing human faces (4). Male children demonstrate more aggressive play at eight, thirteen, and twenty-seven months of age (4). Females exhibit greater language development by thirteen months of age, prefer more highly complex stimuli, and have greater stimulus-field dependency, while males have more finely tuned visual perception and visual–spatial ability (5).

Female biological differences (which some claim make women inferior) include a smaller physical structure and a less fully developed spatial orientation than those of males.

Both folk and scientific dogmas regarding aggression in infants contain some erroneous premises and conclusions. Some researchers have concluded that males are somewhat more aggressive because of the male hormone testosterone. In addition, there have been claims that males are more aggressive because they have a Y chromosome and females do not. There is no substantial experimental evidence which proves that sex hormones are directly responsible for the sexual dimorphism of aggression or assertion (6). Money (6) believes that woman have historically been subordinate to men because men impregnate and women menstruate, gestate, and lactate. Becoming pregnant and having infants to breast-feed decreased the mobility of women throughout the history of the human race, making them more sedentary than men. Only exceptions and exceptional women would break out of this mold. Accordingly, cultural history was grafted onto biological roots.

The biology of women influences female psychology in many ways. Childbearing, a role exclusive to women, should be distinguished from the role of child rearing, which depends on culture. The smaller and weaker physique of women has potential impact on their psychological development. Additionally, the female's sexual organ is less prominent than the male's. This plays a role in sexual attitudes (7), in that the woman does not have a visible organ to seize, name, and direct.

Social Variables in Early Years

While there are many relevant perspectives from which to view the impact of the environment on the person, this discussion is limited to sex-differentiated socialization due to parental rearing.

Sex-differentiated parental interactions with infants are present even in the first year of life. Mothers have been observed to be more responsive and attentive to signals from male infants than from female infants (8). Both mothers and fathers are more responsive to the vocalization of infant sons than to that of infant daughters. These differences in responses of parents continue through the childhood years. For example, it has been shown in a number of studies at several age levels that boys receive more negative feedback, including physical punishment, and yet also receive more positive feedback (9).

Studies have indicated different ways in which parents interact physically with their children. Mothers more frequently stretch the limbs of their three-week-old boys than those of their girls at the same age; they more often imitate sounds made by the girls than by the boys (10). In one direct observational study, mothers held their five-month-old daughters more than the same-aged sons. At age thirteen months, these same daughters were more reluctant to move away from their mothers. Also, the style of play for these same thirteen-month-old children was different. When a barrier was placed in front of them, the boys would more often attempt to get around it by crawling to the end, while the girls would sit where they had been placed and cry. There was a different response and play style with toys as well: boys would tend to throw toys about, while girls tended to gather them together (11).

There is additional evidence that boys and girls are treated differently from the first day of life. Mothers of newborn daughters talked to their infants more, smiled at them more, and physically stimulated them more during feedings than did mothers of newborn sons (12). Moreover, it was observed that mothers talked more to their daughters than their sons throughout infancy. Mothers disciplined their older female infants more by withdrawal of affection and disciplined boys more often by physical punishment (12). Infant boys appear to be given more physical stimulation than girls. They are aroused more frequently from rest, and receive more stimulation to perform gross motor activity. They are also stimulated to perform more varied behaviors than infant girls (13).

It appears that boys are given a greater variety of toys than girls. Their toys afford more inventive possibilities, provide more explicit feedback physically, and encourage manipulation (14). The traditional examples are dolls for girls, who can perform as tender caretakers, and balls and machines for boys, who can manipulate them actively. Girls' toys are more likely to encourage imitation or to be used in close proximity to the caretaker, and do not promote as much opportunity for innovation and variation (15).

In a comprehensive review of the influence of differential socialization in the personality development of males and females, Block (9) discussed several studies involving parental childrearing. In several independent samples, the child-rearing emphasis of both mothers and fathers on achievement and competition parameters was higher for sons than for daughters. Both mothers and fathers encouraged their sons more than their daughters to control the expression of affect (e.g., not to cry), to be independent, and to assume greater personal responsibility. They likewise employed punishment more with sons than with daughters. In relation to their sons, fathers appeared more authoritarian, more physically punishing, less tolerant of aggression, and less tolerant of behaviors outside the traditional gender stereotype. The parental emphasis in rearing daughters was characterized by greater warmth and physical closeness, greater expectation of gentle and "ladylike" behavior, and a hesitancy to use physical punishment. Mothers tended to more greatly restrict and to more closely supervise the activities of their daughters.

Most research studies find that girls receive more pressure to be obedient, responsible, and nurturant, while boys receive more pressure to achieve and be self-reliant. Differential assignment of household chores also reflects a discrepancy: boys are given chores that take them away from the mother and out of the house, whereas girls are assigned tasks that keep them homebound (16). This has been postulated to have some bearing on the greater involvement of women in various social networks and in mutually supportive endeavors, in contrast to the more individualistic activities of men, which emphasize individual mastery (17).

It has been observed that fathers, much more than mothers, exert pressure for sex-appropriate behaviors on both boys and girls (18). Lesser emphasis on achievement and mastery in girls by the father is also reflected in behavior by the mother. Mothers of girls have been observed to provide help in problem-solving situations more than do the mothers of boys (18). This help is provided even when it is not required.

Parents generally make the greatest distinctions between boys and girls in their teachings regarding aggression. Boys are usually permitted and even subtly encouraged to express aggression, while girls are praised for softer, more tender, more caring behavior.

Girls have historically not been taught to compete in sports or other contests, and thus have been denied the early experience of winning and losing gracefully. Girls are conditioned to assert their rights as individuals and defend their persons only in certain passive modalities, such as crying. Girls are encouraged to be less physically active, aggressive, and impulsive, and are forbidden to be as sexually curious and exploratory as boys. The inhibition of natural aggression in girls begins at an early age. Thus they lose some of their freedom to enjoy activities with boys and to move about freely, and are encouraged to spend time enhancing their personal appearance.

There has recently been considerable modification of what has been considered the range of feminine behaviors. Social expectations—until very recently—identified normal femininity as somewhat less assertive, aggressive, and competitive than masculine behavior. These expectations are obvious whether one looks at the names of executives on a corporate ladder or the roster of children's soccer and baseball teams. There is less sense of entitlement for the girl and woman in establishing or achieving personal goals, and greater emphasis on the role of helping others.

For both boys and girls, the intense and complex relationship and interaction during the first two to three years of life is usually primarily with the mother. The father only provides an occasional respite from this intense bond. The relationship of boys and girls to their mother differs in part because boys relate most intensely to a different-sexed parent, while girls have this relationship with a parent of the same sex.

The differences between female and male identification and internal values are related to a variety of factors: biological, developmental, and cultural. If cultural ideals of dependency and docility are incorporated in development, a strong superego will enforce the perpetuation and assertion of these values. A characteristic such as "weakness" or "compliance" thus represents a particular value which has been presented, identified with, and extolled by others, rather than a deficiency when compared to the "strength" of men. If parents have certain values, the daughter will fear loss of love in her earliest years if she does not comply with them. This fear will insure the internalization of these values.

Parents' conscious and unconscious needs and attitudes are reflected in a child. To obtain and retain the parents' love and respect makes the child conform to the image that achieves love and respect. If a girl sees her mother as passive and deferential, or helpless and vulnerable, then assertive and expansive behavior would represent a contradiction of the mother and engender the possibility of losing maternal support. Without support from her mother, the daughter's striving toward independence may become unconsciously equated with aggressive and competitive impulses, and thus produce guilt and anxiety. If particular occurrences make aggression more pronounced—such as severe parental spankings or intense rivalry with siblings—aggression may be equated with punishment or retaliation. Aggressiveness and assertiveness might then be inhibited due to their unconscious equation with punishment.

At a defensive level, the mother who has difficulty dealing with aggression and needs to have a reaction-formation to aggression herself can tolerate only such repression or suppression of aggression within her daughter. So the daughter may, for example, cry when she feels angry, like her mother does. This molding by the mother, and modeling and identification by the daughter, are complementary.

The evidence suggests that the differential response to sons and daughters has some obvious implications for later development, and must be considered in understanding the underlying motivation for adult thought, affect, and behavior. Sex-differentiated socialization practices obviously influence the cognitive development and belief systems of males and females. A socialization process for females which discourages exploration, circumscribes expected spheres of endeavor, and restricts experiences will affect most children. Piaget (19) reminds us that "each time one prematurely teaches a child something that he [she] could have discovered for him [her] self, the child is kept from inventing it and consequently from understanding it completely." This statement needs no amplification or scientific validation. Moreover, it is something that therapists should keep in mind about patients.

There also appears to be subtle emphasis in the ways in which boys are encouraged to be curious and to explore. Curiosity and exploration are associated with superego issues, but also encompass an element of danger, both real and fantasied. Men and women are directed toward somewhat different ideals with respect to curiosity. Girls are not strongly encouraged toward self-sufficiency and are encouraged not to be ashamed of fear—even to bear this trait as a badge of distinction at times. Boys, conversely, may be required to suppress fear.

To fully develop cognitive structures one must encourage, from a very early age, curiosity, exploration of the environment, and independence. Restriction in child-rearing practices lessens the opportunity for experimentation, active engagement, and efforts at mastery. Block (19) elaborates:

> Sex-differentiated socialization practices influence the cognitive development of males and females in several ways that separately and in summation provide more opportunity for independent problem-solving in a variety of contexts for males than for females. The differential provision for the two sexes to engage actively in the world outside the familiar and protected home environment is seen as creating different premises about the world, as developing different competencies, and as reinforcing the use of different cognitive heuristics for dealing with new experiences.

One of the classic examples of impediments to achievement emerged from a longitudinal study of gifted children which began in 1921. The study revealed that the girls were the more gifted artistically, and the most gifted writers were all girls. As adults, all of those gifted children who had become eminent writers and artists were men. About half of the men were professionals in high-level occupations. However, only 11 percent of the women had become professionals, primarily teachers. The most notable achievement of many of the women was their selection of mates, most of whom were achievers (20).

The child has a need for information to distinguish differences: e.g., sexual identity. A crucial issue is the ability to distinguish sexual identity and not blur the differences, while being able to develop a flexible set of behaviors (sex role) unconstrained by stereotyped expectations. Extreme or constricting sex-stereotyped roles and behavior can exist. At another extreme can be the minimization or obfuscation of differences between the sexes. That a boy is no less a boy because he cries and a girl is no less a girl because she plays soccer are important messages we might communicate, and these messages will be internalized and incorporated by the developing individual.

There are also many agents of early socialization outside the nuclear family which have not been discussed but which clearly have impact: school, peers, television, books, and significant others, such as teachers.

Social Variables in Adulthood

The choice of work or career may be more difficult for the young woman than for the young man. The earliest internalized conflicts regarding autonomy will reemerge most profoundly at this nodal point in development. The more traditionally oriented the young woman's family, the more potential there will be for difficulty in resolving these issues. Internal and external conflicts will arise from the intersection of past expectations with contemporary situations and demands. Similarly, there may be conflicting messages from significant others. Parents, teachers, siblings, peers—all may wish the young woman to do well but may unconsciously have expectations based on an earlier context. The problems and contradictions coming from inside may be encouraged by the contradictory values from the outside.

For example, the professional woman who appears to be highly successful in her career may be surprised and perplexed to discover she has a strong desire to have children. Or the mother with two small children may discover she has a desire to work outside the home. Many values, internal and external, impinge on these situations.

Until the last decade, women who strayed from conventional attitudes and images created a disruption of the expected order of things. Society cannot have been reformed so entirely in ten years, because society is composed of individuals with deeply rooted beliefs, ideas, and ideals, as well as conscious and unconscious views of themselves. It is said that when Claire Booth Luce was praised by a colleague for "thinking like a man," she rejected the "compliment" because she felt that thought has no sex. One either thinks or one does not. It has been difficult for society to reconcile the fact that there is no intrinsic masculinity in medicine, business, and law, just as there is no necessary departure from femininity attached to ambition, accomplishment, and success.

In discussing the potential of women, Mannes (20) states a variation on this theme: "Nobody objects to a women's being a good writer or sculptor or geneticist *if*, at the same time, she manages to be a good wife, a good mother, good-looking, good-tempered, well-dressed, well-groomed, and *unaggressive*." There are those even in current society who believe, as Rousseau did several centuries ago, that "a woman's dignity consists of being unknown to the world; her glory is in the esteem of her husband; her pleasures in the happiness of her family." Don José de la Luz, a Cuban educator and poet, calls women "Sun of the house, Moon of the world." According to this view the woman, in her home, generates and radiates her own light; she is a source of warmth, energy, and life. Outside her home, however, she shines only as a reflection of men's burning lights, to be admired and praised by poets, musicians, and lovers. She would, according to this notion, clearly not be an independent person (21).

There have been negative implications and consequences for success by women for many centuries, especially if it involves competitive activity with men. There has been a particular lack of awareness of the extent to which ideas about women's role have shaped our attitudes, and ultimately women's destinies, because these ideas can be so subtle. Some aspects are not so subtle, however. Aristotle believed that women did not become bald because they did not use the contents of their head.

Epstein (22) has pointed out that the small number of women who have achieved considerable success makes it seem as if these women are anomalies, and perhaps pathological. She adds that the argument which states that women pose unfair competition to men, the providers for their families, has the impact of assigning women to supporting roles.

The external restraints and pressures militating against achievement for women in general are secondary to the *perception* of these restrictions and their effect on character formation and self-definition. One woman may see these limitations as insurmountable, and another as challenges to overcome. A more primary role is played by the vicissitudes of development—not only the very crucial early years of life, but continuing development, especially along the lines of separation–individuation, the development of the sense of self, and sexual identity. There still may be subtle social directives that denigrate achievement, adventure, and expansiveness for the girl or woman. There may be pressures and implications directing her to consider what can best be done for the benefit, support, and nurturance of "others," often to the detriment of her own needs. The pleasing attitude of wishing to do "the right things" implies a supportive and nurturant role rather than a role which entails autonomy, creativity, and responsibility. A woman must overcome additional obstacles in order to achieve personal or professional success. In addition to the kinds of anxiety that may be experienced internally in various ways about succeeding, women may have to cope with the additional disapproval of society, of their families, and perhaps especially of their husbands. Anxiety about competition and achievement-striving in men is considered *de rigueur*, but women must justify and explain their need to strive and succeed in a public arena.

Both external obstacles and women's own internal obstacles make it difficult for them to realize their full potential. The repressed rage that may result from their frustrations as they take steps to advance can be psychologically and physically costly. A change in characterological emphasis from compliance and restricted assertiveness to a more expansive style may be accompanied by anxiety and turmoil, manifested in a number of different ways. The manifestations may be solely internal, in the form of psychosomatic symptoms, or may be acted out externally, for example, in the marital arena.

A professor at a major women's college recently indicated that women seeking advice a generation ago were those wanting to enter a profession. She indicated that today the women most apt to feel "peculiar and vaguely unjustified" are those who want to marry and begin a family and are not interested in a career.

Some women feel that the antithesis of the role of a woman is being wife, mother, and nurturer, a stereotype no less tyrannical than one of personal fulfillment being found only in the active pursuit of a career. This posture degrades the career of motherhood to the status of a burdensome hobby.

A desire to be expansive and develop a career may make some women feel uncertain and susceptible, especially if they have a deeply rooted equation of femininity and domesticity.

Empathic reason has only recently prevailed over the momentum of centuries in our view of women and the behaviors expected of them. Reason has been promoted by the public lamentations of a few: the women's suffrage movement politically, psychoanalysts Clara Thompson and Karen Horney, and the feminist movement of the last two decades.

Women are now more broadly accepted in the professional, political, and business world. Birth control and hence freedom from unchosen childbearing, sexual freedom, and liberation from daily tasks which require male physical strength have all changed women's roles. The determined efforts by women to bring about social, legal, economic, and other changes have been increasingly effective. The woman who has a career as well as major matrimonial and maternal responsibilities experiences considerable stress. This stress may cause a regression into gender-stereotype behaviors (23).

Women are increasingly recognizing that the heretofore unquestioned "entitlement" of a husband and father for time away or time alone without parental responsibility is a privilege that does not extend to the wife and mother. And some men are also becoming increasingly aware of the demands on a woman of a dual career. Until recently, men have generally taken major steps in shaping their careers and lives with little conflict, assuming that the role of the woman, the wife, the mother, is to follow. But attitudes are evolving, and decisions about the relationship of job and job location to family life are now becoming more egalitarian.

The process of socialization that makes it acceptable for women to bear the brunt of the responsibility for running a household begins early, as little girls learn to help take care of themselves and others in the home. Little boys are not given the same amount of responsibility, but the inequality sweeps more broadly than menial household tasks or even social issues. Gender-role distinction and identification with the mother establish norms for the developing self-concept of the girl.

Nevertheless, it is no longer manifest destiny that a woman bear a child, nor does her decision not to have one reveal a neurotic difficulty in fulfilling her reproductive potential. The joy of motherhood is as important for some as freedom from becoming a mother is for others. Internal conflict and neurotic mechanisms may be at work in some who decide to have or not to have a child. Personal accomplishment in areas outside the home may be more valued than the desire to have children. The obligatory "pleasing" of the husband as a first priority has been reexamined by many.

Intellectual creativity, work, and a career are available to women *instead of* or *in addition to* the traditional female role of wife and mother. Much of the creative and artistic potential in a woman is often channeled into motherhood. As Greenacre (24) states: "Certainly there is superb artistic creativity involved in the sound rearing of a child." There are certainly new pathways for feminine fulfillment, new possibilities for excelling made available through evolving educational and social opportunities for self-expression. With new opportunities and responsibilities, new conflicts and problems may also become evident.

Identification is composed in part of imitation of another, motivated by the belief that by acting like a powerful and admired parent, one acquires that parent's properties of power and esteem oneself. In addition, shaping by the parents occurs, and there is reward, lack of response, or punishment for certain actions, including those which are "sex-role appropriate." Thus identification, shaping, and observation of live models of the parents all determine what is seen to be "appropriate" behavior for one's sex. This template of acceptability (and stereotype) is then generalized to other aspects of life. Differentially appropriate behavior, and the modeling which goes with it, is imparted not only by the real figures of the parents but by symbolic figures such as those publicized in the media. This model inculcated by parents and others serves as a present—and, by internalization—future reference.

An individual's hopes to acquire, through imitation of a model, the power and positive regard of others can manifest clinically as identification with an aggressor. In situations of an intimidating, overly punitive, harsh, or abusive parent, identification with this parent is often very strong and pervasive. There is motivation to participate in that power to neutralize the traumatic experience and to bring about equality. This same phenomenon has been described among hostages who began to adopt characteristics and goals of their captors. A prisoner, slave, or minority group member comes to accept or even espouse a depreciated view of his/her status to insure maximum security and protection. After a period of subjugation, the people who were subjugated are reluctant to recognize and examine the assumptions they held concerning their lack of privilege and power.

It has been pointed out that women may share with men in ambivalence about women's involvement in the social and professional world (25). Women's participation, work, and involvement are often devalued by ignoring both the contribution and its effect. Each party, the ignorer and the woman ignored, joins in the devaluation.

Why would there be occasional collusion by both men and women to render activities unrecognized or inaccessible? The cultural ambivalence about women's competence is present in at least one if not both sexes at various times. The shaping of the girl and woman toward affection-seeking and passive interests may become a major investment. Some negative social elements arising from roles, mores, and suppression by men are complemented, in some instances, by men who are afraid of a regressive pull toward an infantile position from a controlling and powerful woman who is unconsciously equated with Mother. The first relationship, being symbiotic and with the mother, localizes parental power in only one sex. Dinnerstein (26) notes that the subordination of women may be a function of a desperate need for the male to escape from the all-powerful mother, who is the creator of his world. Rebellion against the perceived power of the mother produces a fear and resentment which can create a subjugation of women to the rule of men, corresponding to the escape from the symbiotic first relationship to the mother. This theory would hold that the attribution by a man of envy, passivity, weakness, and inferiority to women is a defensive reaction against the man's unconscious recollection of his own original weakness and inferiority as a boy in relation to a powerful woman: his mother (27).

Movement into new areas and opening of new vistas creates both opportunity and anxiety, individually and collectively. Comparisons exist not only between men and women, but between women and women as well. Ambivalence about competition with other women who are capable and assertive may bring into awareness conflicts about success-striving. There is some evidence that women sometimes actively limit other women's possibilities for success. The "sisterhood" is a strong force which is evident; other opposing influences also exist.

Many previous barriers have largely fallen during the past decade. Although overt sex discrimination has diminished on many fronts, it may have simply gone underground to emerge in more subtle ways. For example: Why do most women not tell jokes in our culture? Women are somehow expected to listen to and laugh at jokes rather than tell them. There is a social hierarchy which somehow dictates that women fulfill the expectations of receiving and supporting jokes rather than taking the more aggressive joke teller's posture. The lowering or removal of overt barriers to women may be only a role for some to play, while old attitudes and stereotypes are suppressed but not eliminated. Conversations of men at business meetings, at lunchtime, and in the locker room confirm that social change does not produce parallel *internal change*.

It is probably true that women in this country today are freer to pursue their own goals and live independently than in any other country in the world; it is also true that women are still discriminated against in some situations regardless of their ability or skill. These discriminations may range from the subtle to the very blatant. These issues have been well chronicled, and while they serve as a historical as well as current backdrop, they are not the focus of this book. There may indeed be some real situations which, socially speaking, focus or enhance inferiority, but it is my clinical experience that for women who experience inferiority feelings most acutely, the nucleus of these feelings existed internally before finding expression in a cultural setting. It is often assumed that it is because of men and their privileged position that this situation exists, and resentment is then directed toward men. Indeed, the predominant cultures of the Western Hemisphere have been based for many centuries on a patriarchal system. Through the centuries, only particularly clever women or those in special circumstances have been able to circumvent these "givens." Family training has focused on containing women's expectations, with self-expression geared toward rearing of children and other domestic duties.

The emancipation of women, both sexually and socially, is a strain for some, especially in traditional marriages. The conflict in marriage for a woman may occur because of her central role as the one on whom other family members' needs and interests converge, or because of her own individual needs for independence and self-expression. A woman with two careers pays a higher price than a man. Men seem to be able to compartmentalize much better than do women. If her child is ill a woman may be preoccupied during the hours of her outside career no matter how good the caretaking arrangements are. A man is often able to set aside the problems and attend to business-as-usual.

Theories of sex differences have always abounded. Aristotle saw women as partial men, defined by both quantitative and qualitative deficiencies. Pythagoras portrayed the feminine as the second of two opposing principles, as in expressive–receptive, active–passive. Women were defined in terms of men's needs in religious literature and social writings. Jung conceptualized the feminine as one pole of a masculine–feminine polarity of each human psyche, with the feminine as an important element in man's as well as woman's psyche. Woman as partial and deficient man, characterized by what is missing anatomically—a lack which was supposed to greatly affect her emotional organization—was elaborated by Freud at the turn of the century.

There are still differing attitudes toward aggression and assertiveness in men and women. Aggression in women is sometimes seen by both women and men as a "bad" trait, inconsistent with the ideal women have of themselves. This ideal may, in part, have to do with their own mothers, who may have had difficulty asserting themselves and who needed to inhibit this expression in themselves as well as their daughters. Women who have been systematically taught that it is desirable to please others and conform to the expectations of others have particular difficulty in this area. At the extreme is the woman who is raised to be pleasing, nonassertive, generous to others even to the point of emotional martyrdom; she is dependent, possibly timid, and centered only on family. Perhaps the only acceptable way of expressing aggression is passively. In the play *Death Trap* the wife tells her husband: "I'm just going to stay down here with you when your colleagues arrive so that you can worry if I am going to say something bizarre."

Another example of the socially acceptable way to show or express certain feelings or issues is for the woman to cry rather than get angry. Crying as the epitome of reaction-formation against aggression is demonstrated by a nineteenth-century story. The husband would not give the wife something she wanted despite her repeated requests, whereupon the wife and her daughter colluded to weep profusely whenever he appeared. This occurred for several weeks until the father finally could stand it no longer and gave in.

Men may actually prefer women for what they are not, rather than what they are. Sharing life with someone who has her own views, sees clearly, and has her own needs to satisfy is very threatening to some men. It may be in some cases threatening for the man to be subordinate to a woman in his professional or business life. This situation may reverberate with his own subordination as a little boy to a powerful woman, his mother, and recapitulate unresolved conflict and affect.

If women were in fact biologically inadequate, unworthy, or ambitious beyond their capacities, men would not need to spend so much time and effort in ridicule and resistance. Shakespeare might have captured this dynamic by stating "The man doth protest too much."

Aggressiveness in women may be mistakenly regarded as the inability to accept femininity. There is no doubt that there are aggressive women, just as there are aggressive men. Assertiveness is a comfortable and acceptable way to express the basic drive of aggression that is common to everyone. The question is, how comfortable is one with it, i.e., is it the manifestation of conflict or the product of a healthy and sublimated drive? If it is conflictually driven and associated with anxiety, there may be such associated behaviors as belligerence, inappropriate assertiveness of a compulsive nature, or even a militant posture.

The female role model is currently different from past standards. This cultural alteration means that the measurements women previously used to determine their success in life may not be applicable in the later decades of the twentieth century. Success for a woman today may be clearly different from that of her mother's generation. In earlier years the female was divorced from political, economic, and sociological problems. The prevailing cultures limited her significance to the kitchen and bedroom. Her role was determined by the combination of being a mother and being completely dependent on the male, both economically and physically.

Feminine "masochism," rather than being a female tendency toward passivity, could be reviewed as the culminating characteristic of a number of forces impinging on the woman to turn her naturally occurring aggressiveness inward, if she finds its expression unacceptable socially or emotionally.

A restatement of female psychology, especially in reconciling activity, aggressiveness, and self-assertiveness with femininity, would have to be made with the simple observation that creative, competitive, and successful women can also possess "feminine" qualities of gentleness, serenity, receptiveness, and gratifying sexuality.

SECTION II

Developmental Aspects
of Achievement

CHAPTER 2

The Concept of Gender

THE OUTCOME OF THE NEGOTIATIONS of early developmental tasks and processes establishes a set of expectations for future mastery and achievement. One perspective from which to view precursors of achievement/inhibition is that of developmental lines and phases. Particular attention will be paid in this and the following chapters to the developmental lines of gender identity, sexual identity, and narcissism. In addition, these chapters will explore separation–individuation, Oedipal, and adolescent phases and their relationship to the adult woman's ability to achieve.

The development of a girl's *gender identity* (the concept of maleness or femaleness) and *sexual identity* (the concept of femininity or masculinity) begins between ages two and five and continues well into adulthood. After about twenty-four months of age it is almost impossible to change gender identity; the only re-formation which can occur is surgical and hormonal alignment of anatomical gender to correspond with internal identity (i.e., sex-reassignment surgery for transsexuals). The basic imprint of gender is a preverbal, conflict-free identification that cannot be altered by therapeutic intervention. The early-established gender sense becomes a foundation on which sexual identity and self-identity are built. The majority of these issues precede the Oedipal phase (ages three to six).

New experiences become integrated around and within existing perceptions of the self, gender, and sexual identity. A new experience is generally valued more highly when it fits an already existing scheme. Thus boys value male activities and attributes and girls value female activities and attributes. The little girl will state, "I want to do this (and be) like Mommy, because I'm a girl like her."

The early foundation for those values forming the core of sexual identity occurs around ages three to six. It is at this age that the boy or girl begins to observe and imitate the same-sexed parent. The young child views what is and is not a part of the accepted behavior and attitude of his/her model. The girl observes and senses the mother's activity and comfort with that activity. She has some early sense of the expansiveness or constraint of the mother, of what tasks the mother performs, and of her manner of relating to everyone in the household. She learns if it is more acceptable by her mother as well as her father and siblings if she plays house or football. She perceives values attributed to herself, her mother, and other women by her father. She senses who the father plays with first and most: herself or her brother. Boys may also have established at this age some basic ideas about the appropriateness of sensitivity, tenderness, crying, or other open expressions of feeling and caring for others, and they may have observed the division of domestic duties and responsibilities.

The sex that is attributed to an infant during the initial two years of life (e.g., even if a biological male might be reared as a girl) plays the most important role of all possible variables, including genetic, hormonal, and anatomical factors, in the establishment of gender identity (2). Several infants who have been studied had ambiguous external genitalia, and some, because of hormonal problems, appeared anatomically to be the opposite of their genetic and internal sex. Each of these children developed along the line of rearing: that is, a child who had been reared as a female during the first two years of life would establish a *gender identity* of *female*, regardless of biological, genetic sex. The conclusion from these studies is that the sex of rearing—i.e., the psychological elements—is more dominant than a combination of genetic, anatomical, and hormonal components in establishing an internal sense of gender. In the study of transsexuals, the importance of psychological factors in the first two years of life is crucial. To date there has been no demonstration that there are genetic, constitutional, hormonal, or physiological factors which cause transsexualism. By the end of the second year of life, if the internal sense of gender identity is female—regardless of the external anatomy—that sense of femaleness will remain throughout life (3).

Although transsexuals who are biologically and anatomically female but believe themselves to be really male are much rarer than biological males who believe they are really female (the ratio of anatomical male transsexuals to anatomical female transsexuals is 8:1), some studies have been made of these cases (4). The findings indicate that during the first year of life, the mother-infant symbiosis is usually severely disrupted. One cause for this disruption can be a severe depression in the mother, such that she is unable to take care of her daughter. No one acts as a mother-surrogate, as would be the case if the mother had died. Hence the infant is given only subsistence mothering. This creates an unusual dilemma for the infant girl in that her mother may be physically present but is emotionally out of reach. A common trait in female transsexuals is a lifelong urge to protect very feminine-appearing and mothering women. This behavior can be seen as a result of the severe deprivation of mothering in infancy. Frequently, the little girl, in the emotional absence of the mother, establishes a reasonably good relationship with the father as she turns to him for care and closeness. In most cases of this kind, the father does not support the wife's suffering; rather, he envisions his daughter as the succorer. The father encourages behavior in his daughter like his own; that is, he encourages masculinity and fosters a male identity. By the age of three or four the girl feels herself to be male (gender identity) and acts in many ways like a little boy (sexual identity). Usually by this age she is dressing in boys' clothes, playing boys' games, and imagining herself to have a penis, and she may even pray to God nightly to have one affixed (3).

In less extreme cases, some aspects of an inadequate mother-daughter symbiosis—with a mother who is at times unreachable and unempathic, combined with turning to the father for empathic support—produce the pathological constellation found in women that has been called "masculine protest" or marked "penis envy."

Research indicates an opposite situation with male transsexuals. In remarkably sensitive research, Stoller has found that many male transsexuals had an excessively close and all-too-gratifying intimacy with their mothers in which there was no disruption for at least the first two years of life. Stoller (5) states:

> There is reason to believe, therefore, just as excessively close and gratifying mother/son intimacy can produce femininity even in a biologically intact male, so can massive disruption of symbiosis cause masculinity in a female child; just as a psychologically absent father can contribute to femininity in a boy, so can a close relationship based on identification with father (rather than on father as a heterosexual object) contribute to masculinity in a girl; and, just as a mother who encourages graceful and non-masculine behavior in a boy can contribute to his femininity, so can reinforcing non-feminine masculine behavior by a father encourage masculinity in a girl. (p. 72)

From these studies of transsexualism, it appears that both female gender identity and feminine sexual identity are more secure in the girl's basic identification with mother than are the same identifications in the boy. As was mentioned before, females in the mother-infant relationship have their earliest links with someone of the same sex. Normal mother-child symbiosis enhances a girl's identification with the female, whereas in males it can represent a feared position of regression. The girl emerges, usually after the third year of life, as a distinct and separate person psychologically from the mother. If this early symbiosis is defective, inadequate, or ruptured, the girl is vulnerable to searching continuously for a good mother, in lavish, longing fantasy, in overt homosexual affairs, or in transsexualism.

Parental gender assignment and rearing appear to far outweigh combined biological factors in the composite of learning by identification, modeling, and imitation, via both parents, as well as through parental conditioning of behavior in determining gender identity (6).

The gender concept of maleness or femaleness, established by age two, exists long before the discovery of the genitals, and its early development does not seem related to growth of the sexual drive (7).

Stoller (5) conceptualizes two orders or types of development of "femininity" in women. In the first, he postulates a conflict-free period in which a little girl imitates, models, identifies with, and is taught by the mother. From this are developed ideas, attitudes, and fantasies about her basic self and basic sexuality which can be termed *gender identity*. The manifestations of this phase of development are such external and culture-bound behaviors as the way the little girl carries herself, the clothes she prefers, and the dolls or games she enjoys. It also gives rise to such qualities as the wish to be a mother, to nurse and cuddle a baby, or to raise and educate a child, as she experiences her own mother doing. If the early bonds with her mother are interrupted or are unempathic, then the thrust may be toward a *disidentification* with her mother, and an urge to be as unlike her mother as possible, including remaining childless. (This will be discussed at greater length later.)

The second order of femininity has its origins in the Oedipal situation, generally between ages three and six. This phase of development focuses on affection, on awareness of sexual anatomical differences, and perhaps on a wish for children, depending on the identification bond with the mother. This second order of femininity, then, results from conflict and envy in the Oedipal situation and gives rise via perceptions and fantasy creations to solutions to these problems. This universal Oedipal phenomenon, which is largely unconscious, does not imply that psychopathology is an inevitable result, but only that for some who have developmental difficulties a pathological *resolution* at this phase is possible. The normal varieties of this phase give depth and richness to the unique development of the woman. There is a new desire for (and a certain fear of) affection as well as awareness of anatomical differences between the sexes. As the little girl switches from allegiance to her mother to yearning for her father, creative tension will fashion conscious and (largely) unconscious fantasies: for example, fantasies of surpassing Mother in getting Father's attention and becoming the object of his desire. These fantasy solutions are conceived to reverse the frustrations and perhaps trauma of reality; they are an ultimate defense against being little and relatively helpless. Thought, play, and family scenarios in the girl's mind will be constructed around the satisfaction of her fantasies. What the father likes and finds attractive, and what he reinforces, are all very carefully sensed as she gathers in clues at many different levels from her environment and shapes them into her own development and behavior. The behaviors which work, feel good, and are perhaps reinforced become repeated and eventually more ingrained as a component of character structure.

It is important to note that primary and secondary femininity, arising from different processes, can be independent of each other. For example, a woman may appear very "unfeminine" in demeanor yet be an exemplary mother. Acquisition of primary femininity is a conflict-free learning experience in which the little girl identifies with or is taught and encouraged by her mother. Mechanisms such as imprinting, conditioning, identification, and imitation contribute heavily and often result in attitudes, convictions, and fantasies that we refer to as "core gender identity." There are culture-bound phenomena which are interwoven, such as the clothes the little girl prefers and the dolls she chooses to play with—as well as the fact that she is playing with a doll instead of a football.

Knowing that she has the capacity to bear children, that she will be able to decide whether or not to do so, are important aspects of self-definition in the development of the girl and woman.

As soon as any behavior appears that can be considered gender-related, little girls can be distinctly feminine in style, language, carriage, and fantasy life. This is in contrast to turn-of-the century definitions, even psychoanalytic definitions, of femininity as a condition characterized by passivity, masochism, and a penis envy that would supposedly be assuaged only by the substitute of growing a baby.

CHAPTER 3

———————

Separation–Individuation Issues

UNRESOLVED SEPARATION–INDIVIDUATION issues may appear in therapy as "success phobia" with unique dynamic underpinnings. The separation–individuation phase of development occurs between ages eighteen and thirty-six months. Separation-individuation is a separate developmental line which is navigated throughout life; "separation" refers not to physical separation but to the psychic phenomenon of experiencing one's self as separate from the mother. Individuation is an intrapsychic process, with the attainment of self-regulation and individual autonomy beginning by about the second year and coursing throughout life. The separation–individuation process is a continuing one which is reworked incrementally at each successive stage of development—including adolescence—but its successful resolution is predicated on adequate negotiation of these issues by the end of the third year of life (1).

Several steps of separation–individuation are to be attained in the progression from infancy to adulthood: the increasing psychological and physical separation from primary need–gratifying persons, such as the parents; the associated internal representation of the parents so that they need not be physically present;

and a sense of intrapsychic organization in the development of the sense of self so that structures, boundaries, motivation, and other such related qualities are now *internal* rather than external. When the mother cannot accept the child's separation, especially if her own anxiety about separation is an unresolved conflict, she may foster an overly intense bond between herself and her child. The goal of individuation as an achievement of autonomy of a child's function in a gradual manner may become thwarted. Individuation—including adaptation developmentally to relinquish dependence on people, especially Mother, for supply and feedback—may be impeded. This can affect the child's ability to master new experiences and limit the full development of her potential.

Mahler (1) has demonstrated that when the mother-infant symbiotic phase of development is unpredictable, painfully frustrating rather than satisfying the needs of the child—or, alternatively, marked by too much exclusiveness, since the mother cannot accept the child's separation—the result may be separation panic, dread of dissolution of the self, and fear of loss of identity. The step of separation–individuation is then experienced as a catastrophic threat.

The freedom to discover and pursue novel solutions without disrupting a stable sense of well-being or safety, the ability to independently and comfortably depart from stereotyped and automatic responses to internal and external demands, as well as giving up reliance on a structured environment, are part of the development process of autonomy. Individuation is an adaptive aspect of development which includes giving up infantile needs and concomitant dependence on others for narcissistic supplies. The acquisition of increasing mastery and experience creates new potentialities which allow relinquishment of a dependent posture. The adaptive process of individuation requires the renunciation of earlier needs and relationships with people as only need-meeting functions, so that pleasure and mastery may be experienced through independent activity in constantly evolving achievements.

For individuation and separation to occur successfully, the child must experience security and support for her increasing self-expression and mastery. Some parents, however, react to the child's natural moves toward independence as though the child were abandoning them or competing with them. The child experiences feelings of insecurity and rejection, and/or hostility, along with a competitive struggle for control and supremacy. It is as if the parents are somehow threatened by the girl's new attempts at independence; the child who is feeling precariously good about these attempts is particularly vulnerable to negative parental reactions and will come to feel insecure and anxious rather than pleased about her normal growth processes. Such a child may strive toward mastery and independence, but her self-assertion and successes are likely to become unconsciously confused with her aggressive and competitive impulses, thus becoming associated with guilt and anxiety.

When the parent(s) disallow progressive emotional separation, the girl may have to take an extreme position, such as adolescent rebellion, or settle for a compromised success, complying with the (largely unconscious) parental need for stymied emancipation, rather than face the loss of love of her parents. The young child is unable to make fine distinctions among the parents' negative reactions, so her ambivalence about and fear of accomplishment are likely to be generalized to most endeavors rather than limited to specific activities. This is, then, one type of parent-child interaction which may give rise to fear of success: the independence-inhibiting part of the interaction. All the while, parents will have and express conscious wishes that their children should grown and mature and become independent.

The child, in the face of these inconsistent messages, is likely to be confused and ambivalent. Her attempts at growth and mastery produce a certain amount of anxiety and insecurity, especially as success or recognition are about to be consummated. There are a number of strategies or psychological defenses that may help her deal with fear of success or reduce the uncomfortable feeling of anxiety associated with undertaking tasks leading to independence and competence. One strategy involves shifting attention and concern to peripheral aspects of the tasks, or avoiding completion of the tasks entirely. A related strategy involves acquiring a disparaging view of oneself as an inadequate performer. These strategies keep the performer deflected from competence and independence-producing aspects of the task being undertaken.

The anxiety and insecurity initially produced by negative parental reactions to the child's autonomy and success eventually become internalized and operate independently as "the dictates of conscience." Thus, this early syndrome can be carried to adulthood and manifest itself in many ways.

When the normal separation–individuation process must be accomplished in a pathological and rebellious manner to effect ego differentiation, an internal price is paid. The child is faced with a dilemma of rebelling or succumbing. Passive rebellion is often seen as safer, avoiding the exposure of intense anger and the danger of retaliation. Usually the parental disallowal of individuation is so indirect, unconscious, and seemingly well-intentioned that the child will not allow herself to recognize her rebellious anger, and it remains largely unconscious. The defiant and assertive attempt at self-expression of "I won't" is converted to a helpless and passive "I can't." The child then feels a kind of inadequacy.

When the child feels this helplessness and dependency, she may feel a need to remain tied to her mother. This regressive attempt to prevent separation and individuation may then establish and fashion coping mechanisms, and perhaps a life-style.

Developmentally, anxiety is provoked in the young child when she anticipates the possibility that Mother will not relieve her discomforts. An adequate and optimal sense of frustration is important in that it allows the growing child to differentiate herself from the mother, whereas the failure to allow for adequate experiences of frustration inhibits this differentiation and development and thus ultimately sabotages the separation–individuation process. For example, the mother who continues to provide need-meeting functions for the child when it is no longer appropriate or necessary inhibits independence. This creates an *inhibition of independent assertion*. One of the manifestations of this inhibition may be the phobia-like avoidance of independent assertion, and thereby an inhibition of success as an adult. Manifesting as a "fear of success," or successful completion, this is actually a fear of final separation and autonomy. When the mother spares the child the pain of ordinary experiences of trial and error, the child begins to believe that she is *inadequate*.

Often women with this type of childhood background come to treatment in a panic situation due to the loss of a relationship with a need-meeting person, often a husband, who supported and gratified their every need. These women may describe their relationship as ideal, if not somewhat overprotected, with a person who, like their mother, protected them and "did everything" for them.

This form of "success phobia" is experienced as a threat of abandonment by a primary figure who provides reinforcement of the phobic avoidance of independent assertion and function. Success phobia based on the threat of absence of, or separation from, a primary figure or the equivalent symbolic surrogate of that figure is in essence based on the fear of abandonment, with phobic ideation and consequent avoidance of the phobic situation. The self-imposed constraint of behavior spares the phobic person the threat of abandonment.

In experiments with elementary school children and their parents, the parents of success-fearing children made substantially more critical comments, made more demands and offered more hints, and made more attempts to perform tasks for the children than did the parents of non–success fearing children (2). A child may receive the messages of constant parental interference in one of several ways. For example, she may interpret a parent's participation as more valuable than her own. Or she may feel that the parent does not want her to act independently. She might determine that mistakes are to be avoided at all costs. Most importantly, she will interpret that she is inadequate and incapable of doing the job alone.

Separation from the mother may be experienced as a guilt-ridden act of hostile aggression, with this pre-Oedipal guilt revived with each step toward independence. The unconscious perception of the daughter is that success is achieved at the expense of her mother. Later, as an adult, she may not be able to succeed because it would unconsciously threaten to disrupt the bond with the mother. The price paid is a lack of autonomy, unconscious guilt, or psychosomatic symptoms. The mother in some way transmits the message that total loyalty and allegiance are required if the daughter is to remain in a position of special and favored attention.

To be taken care of by someone else is a role and presents a conflict for some women. I am referring to a broad continuum of dependency: at one end are the ubiquitous wishes to receive and to be cared for; and at the other end of the spectrum is a pathological sense of dependence which is a conflictual need. For the woman at this latter end of the spectrum, to succeed and be more independent and autonomous would paradoxically jeopardize, in her mind, her potential for being taken care of and nurtured. This nurturance may be given by a husband or by a series of supportive friends who function as providers and regulators of both dependency needs and self-esteem. Defects of self-regulation often relate to difficulties in separation–individuation.

A healthy separation–individuation process establishes boundaries and limits within, and the regulation of esteem from within, a kind of self-sufficiency. The sense of self develops consistency by an internalization of the parents' empathic qualities, resulting in a feeling of being understood, accepted, and loved. It is then that the girl may see herself as a person who can be empathically understood as a separate individual from her parents.

The internalization of the mother's empathic quality becomes incorporated into the child's self as an enduring feature with concomitant self-regulatory capacities and self-expression. The structuralization of *self-experience* by means of empathy is a developmental process (3).

An analogy may help illustrate these unconscious processes revealed during therapy and analysis. The developmental thrust of the child is toward mastery, independence, and autonomy within the context of an adequate environment and an empathic parental framework. Yet the matrix of this early experience, at least until about age three, is within a symbiotic union with the mother. Normal development may be likened to Siamese twins who *each* have their own vital organs and have developed to a point of separateness except that one or more minor attachments remain. The surgical procedure to separate them is relatively minor and not life-threatening, and they each subsequently achieve their individual identities and set about their own lives. If the mother has experienced a conflictual separation–individuation process herself, she has an incomplete sense of herself, with desperate feelings of needing someone else to make her feel "whole." The daughter comes along, and their attachment is intense. This "twinship" is emotionally life-supporting for both. Separation of *this* daughter-and-mother dyad can be likened to an attempt to separate Siamese twins in whom several vital organs are shared, and for whom it would be hazardous or deadly to attempt surgical separation. Similarly, in a mother-daughter "twinship," the girl may feel she is taking vital and powerful things away from the mother to achieve her own autonomy. Thus the wish to succeed in the latter type of dyad is unconsciously equated with murderous aggression or retaliation toward her mother. The guilt associated with separation binds her to the mother emotionally and prevents the daughter at this early phase of development from being more autonomous and independent.

Galenson (4) has found in her analytic exploration of examination anxiety in women that the symptoms of examination anxiety are derived from one of three major areas: a fear of object loss (separation anxiety), a fear of loss of bodily integrity, or a fear of genital imperfection. Symptoms in those patients with fear of object loss included the appearance of a sense of detachment and intense loneliness which caused disruption in studying. To repair this loss, the women would feel compelled to establish contact with someone immediately. Also occurring at these times in this group of patients were eating binges, followed by remorse and guilt with subsequent dieting. Bouts of excessive sleep and excessive activity also occurred in some patients in this group. Studying for and taking examinations were both like entering unknown territories of autonomy, which would create anxiety and force a retreat to a more dependent position of personal contact with a friend or family. Although Galenson believes that this group of problems originates in the oral phase of development, the particular struggles of taking steps to autonomy, the need at times for darting back to maternal surrogates for emotional refueling before striking out again on one's own and being "examined" for one's competence in independent functioning is much more reminiscent of the rapprochement subphase of separation–individuation (5).

In Galenson's study, a second group of patients had symptoms clustered around anxiety over total body integrity. At academic examination time in particular, a preoccupying focus of these patients was examination of parts of their own body, which they usually found inadequate or unattractive. Constant self-inspection of some bodily imperfection would ensue. Some patients developed hypochondriacal concerns. These bodily concerns were concurrent with worry about intellectual imperfection or inadequacy: The patients felt that they would fail the exam unless they knew every detail of the subject they were studying. Excess anxiety then caused panic and inability to recall known facts or entities. Galenson equated this level of anxiety with anal issues and conflict: Having to produce answers at a specific time in a prescribed manner was like having to please Mother by producing and performing in a way she demanded.

A third group, which experienced the most developmentally advanced level of anxiety, showed concerns over genital imperfection. The women in this group had a deep fear of being shown to lack something—a feeling that their intellectual phoniness would be revealed. Consistent fantasies were of sexual exploratory "Doctor" games of early childhood, concomitant with a fear of being found to be "without something."

An important aspect of development often overlooked, and only recently receiving attention, is the impact and function of the father from infancy onward. The presence of the father becomes a major factor during the second year of life. He usually supports the child's efforts toward autonomy, helping to prevent reunion with or engulfment by the mother. He may encourage separation from, rather than clinging to, the mother (often more actively in the boy than in the girl). He is an object available for the boy's identification. Evidence of this is seen in psychotic regression among patients with a severe psychopathology. A common delusional or hallucinatory experience in psychotic women is of heterosexual assault and vulnerability, while men's fear of losing their maleness may result in anxieties about being homosexual. From a psychoanalytic developmental standpoint, the sense of maleness, established in the first two to three years of life, and the later development of masculinity, established during the Oedipal period (ages four to five and beyond), is less firmly established and more fragile in males than the sense of femaleness and femininity is in females. This relatively more precarious position in males is due to the primary identification and early symbiosis with a female, the mother. Males must overcome this primary position in relation to their mothers. Most boys and men fear homosexuality much more than do girls. In this context homosexuality represents a feared retreat to a primary position of being feminine. The hostile ridicule of women inherent in a homosexual's effeminate gestures exemplifies the mockery and depreciation of what is feared. (The stylized gestures of some homosexuals are not feminine, but effeminate.) Adolescent boys may have a phase of depreciation of homosexuals in reaction to anxiety about their own adequacy and virility.

The most severe pathology of the separation–individuation phase is the borderline personality disorder, in which there is a lack of self-definition, giving rise to a "false self," experiences of emptiness, and alternating clinging and aloofness. The etiology of the borderline personality disorder has been traced to a particular pattern of interaction between the mother and child, and the pathology focuses on the mother-child relationship originating in the separation–individuation phase, particularly the rapprochement subphase (6, 7). The mother of the future borderline child and adult is herself borderline. She rewards and gratifies her infant in a particular way. The infant is rewarded or given gratification whenever he or she behaves in a dependent and clinging manner. The mother couples this behavior with covert threats to reject or abandon the child if too much effort at independence is made. This threat of rejection or abandonment takes the form of the withdrawing of positive, warm, sustaining emotional responses and approval. The child is thwarted in movement toward separation–individuation, and unconsciously equates autonomy and independence with abandonment and the nonfulfillment of emotional needs. Furthermore, remaining dependent and symbiotic would guarantee the continuance of support, but only at the expense of independence and autonomy. The child, even as an infant, then feels stymied. This conflict between, on the one hand, remaining dependent to insure the needed (at this time) support and nurturance and, on the other hand, growing and losing this support is a dilemma carried unconsciously into adulthood.

The enmeshed borderline mother and the borderline girl exemplify this issue in a vivid manner. Separation for either would be devastating. Independence and success (the success of autonomy in this case) would mean losing functionally a part of the self, for both the girl and the mother. Separation would be the equivalent of "out of sight, out of mind." This malevolent identification is with the mother, and the role of the maternal object in the psychic life of the child is for the mother to focus her desperate needs on the child. Obviously autonomy and its derivatives for the girl suffer.

CASE STUDY: THE RELUCTANT VIOLINIST

The following account of a patient, Nina, will illustrate the struggle with some of the issues just elaborated. Nina came to therapy at age thirty, with an initial complaint of a troubling inability to make significant changes in her life. She was distraught that she had been unable to have the kind of career she wanted and felt capable of achieving. She had a desire to leave her job and begin a business of her own, but felt frightened and not capable.

She had experienced an abiding discomfort with assertiveness and expression of her feelings around co-workers and particularly with superiors. It was readily apparent how agonizing it was for her to comfortably be aware of thoughts or feelings which were either novel or aggressive. She all too readily agreed with any comment or observation which was made to her, and searched for ways to reflect what she thought were the therapist's own views and ideas.

Nina was intelligent, had done well in school, and had a special interest and talent in music. Faced with the choice of accepting a music scholarship at a prestigious school or going to another college with her boyfriend, Hal, she chose the latter. Her relationship with Hal was characterized by hostile dependency. She clung to him, and was terrified of being alone. She and Hal fought much of the time when they were together. Mistrusting her own judgment and succumbing to her fear of being alone, she chose to place her hopes and expectations in the achievements of Hal and identified them as more important than her own goals. In doing so, she in effect relinquished her own goals.

Nina married Hal and supported him through college and graduate school. She had avoided becoming self-sufficient and establishing her own identity by subjugating her independence to her husband. She made efforts at establishing her own separate identity and life, but these were confused and self-defeating, and she was unable to take advantage of the wider opportunity currently available to her. She felt impotent rage over her sense of despair and immobilization in overcomings her feelings of inadequacy. She began to turn her attention to the women's movement for reparation of what she felt men had done to her. Initially in treatment there was unconscious as well as conscious resistance toward individuation and autonomy. The fear of self-emergence, autonomy, and adult responsibility seemed overwhelming at times.

She recalled, "My mother tried to control my emotional reactions, so that I would be automated and predictable. She couldn't handle a free spirit. She's a dead person inside. The thought of being like that to my kids makes me shudder. I have a totally negative identification with my mother; I had recurrent dreams as a child of my mother saying, 'You have to die.' In the dream there would be an open area (I suppose representing freedom) in the distance, and when I reached it I would die; so I never reached it. I have never been able to work as I would like to. I tried to get love from doing a job well, and feel good about myself out of my work, but it never worked out. I'm afraid to take risks—to make any serious commitment. I really want to make use of my degree in music and my talent in violin, but I'm unable to. So far, I have only been able to function at the job I have now, which is boring and not challenging.

"It was like Mother wasn't there psychologically. She was always withdrawing from me. Anger was not acceptable to her. I was so controlled. I am so controlled inside now with my husband and at my work. I am just now realizing how angry I am at her for withdrawing from me. It's like I have a fear of women; maybe it's because I'm so mad at women. I am so undeveloped in certain areas. My passions are in total control."

Nina described a feeling she had when she was around her mother that the mother could not tolerate her being angry. "On the other hand, when I get angry it's like she feels superior. Like it was weak of me to be angry." She elaborated the subtle ways in which her mother discouraged autonomy, while encouraging dependent behavior which enhanced reliance upon her. Nina added, "In some way I was afraid of being harmful to my mother if I asserted myself. I was careful not to feel too much of anything."

Over a course of treatment we traced the origins of these difficulties as they unfolded in her history and in the transference. A particular type of internal configuration emerged. Because of the mother's probably tenuous self-control and incomplete sense of self, a symbiotic relationship with the daughter persisted. The daughter felt that she could not express or even think of ideas or feelings contrary to her mother's. She looked to her mother for confirmation of herself and even of her existence. She felt "not real" and "as if I don't exist unless I get tied in or hooked up with my mother every so often."

It became apparent that the mother would not respond at all to her daughter if affects or behaviors were expressed which were contrary to her own or of which she did not approve. In such cases Nina's mother literally treated her as not being real, or not being there, by refusing to acknowledge or reflect certain aspects of Nina's behavior and emotions. A dual purpose was thus served. The mother created a daughter who was an extension of herself—an extremely "good" daughter who tried harder and harder to please but found the goal of perfection always elusive.

Nina allowed her mother's efforts and desires to replace her own. After Nina achieved something as a girl, she would be left alone and would feel abandoned by her mother. Only when the mother recognized the feeling of aloneness and abandonment would some empathic caretaking be reinstated. Nina was afraid to become angry lest she destroy contact with her mother, knowing that the mother would withdraw in a painful retaliation if she were to become too expressive, particularly expressive of anger.

As she further examined her desire to leave her job and begin her own business, she said, "It's frightening to go into business on my own. It seems so much easier for Hal, because his father was in business and he's sure somehow that he can make a go of it. I feel like any undertaking or change like this is so threatening and I fear the worst, like starving."

She later described a "horrible sense of direction," causing Hal to either take over or direct her. As the therapy progressed, she was able to see that this troubled "sense" was not caused by an innate deficit. In therapy she explored issues of dependency as well as fears of severe consequences for making even a single mistake.

A few months into treatment, she described a dream in which there were clay figures: a male figure over a baby, and in the background a female who had a hole in the back of her head and shoulders where the baby had emerged. The female figure looked quite angry. The baby, Nina concluded, depicted herself, given a new birth into autonomy through psychotherapy, separate from her mother for the first time. Since she was not merged with her mother any longer, she was the object of her mother's anger for having left her. The reciprocal needs of both her mother and herself for each other were recognized; their close interdependence was both wished and feared.

Nina wanted to come to treatment forever. This attempt at avoiding both change and a definitive resolution of her separation–individuation issues would have simply perpetuated both her internal conflict and her perception of herself. She quickly recognized that this wish recapitulated her earlier avoidance of autonomy. She would have simply substituted the therapist for her mother.

As she ended treatment, she reported that she was quite happy with herself and her marriage, no longer experienced depressions, and had a dual career of owning a music store and playing violin in an orchestra. She noted especially that she felt complete, whole, and happy.

CHAPTER 4

Narcissism: Healthy and Pathological

THE DEVELOPING SENSE of self in the child is determined by internal sensations and perceptions which are repeatedly validated by appropriate responses from the mother. The product of these interactions is a cohesiveness of the self forming the foundation of identity. If the mother's responses to the infant's and young child's needs and feelings are not reliable and consistent, however, then the internal sensations and perceptions of the child are not validated or integrated, and no cohesive sense of self can develop (1).

Female children particularly need to experience the mother, and, to a degree the father, as someone who can take on life energetically and competitively. This vitality is helpful not only in the mirroring and empathic matrix which is established in the parent-child unit, but also in establishing a model with whom the child identifies, incorporating this model as an ideal. As the phase-appropriate mirroring of needs and wishes of the child are met, idealization is replaced by identification. To be totally empathic (which is impossible) would prevent the child from experiencing herself as separate. Empathic failures occur, and are part of the optimal frustration of development. When a child has to "come to the parent's side" to remain in contact, however, as opposed to the parent having the empathic ability to come to the child's side, the child then has to abandon her own internal point of reference.

That is, the need of a girl during this developmental phase is for parents to confirm her interests, activities, and identity, rather than refocusing attention on themselves and their own needs and interests. The empathic efforts of the mother to understand affects, behavior, and thinking in the child require the ability to differentiate herself from her young daughter.

Kohut (1) has described how the developmentally immature, "grandiose self" is transmuted during the first two years of life into appropriate and mature self-esteem by parental "mirroring" in which the parents reflect the worth of the child and her full range of affects. Developmentally appropriate loving, encouragement, and empathic responses reflect to the child a view of herself as a worthwhile and valued person who does not need a defensive grandiosity, but can come to have an appropriate and healthy self-esteem.

Phase-appropriate responses of approval, reflection, mirroring, confirmation, and admiration of a child lead to normal maturational steps which transform and internalize grandiosity and exhibitionism into the beginnings of a mature capacity for ambitions, goals, and a cohesive sense of self, including self-esteem. Kohut (2) summarizes the importance of empathy and its function both inside and outside a clinical situation:

> Empathy, the recognition of the self in the other, is an indispensable tool of observation, without which vast areas of human life, including man's behavior in the social field, remain unintelligible. Empathy, the expansion of the self to include the other, constitutes a powerful psychological bond between individuals which more perhaps even than love, the expression of sublimation of the sexual drive, counteracts man's destructiveness against his fellows. Empathy, the accepting, confirming, and understanding human echo evoked by the self, is a psychological nutriment without which human life as we know it and cherish it could not be sustained.

A small child has little awareness of the limitations and distortions that may be imposed upon her by inaccurate and unempathic responses from the parents, and will accept the image of herself reflected from the parents as accurate.

How does this set the stage for achievement or its inhibition? Without the evolution of these early developmental needs for self-confirmation and valuation into a healthy self-esteem, the person must continually look to others and the environment for confirmation and valuation of the self. If others or the environment consistently fail to reflect the longed-for empathic responses, self-esteem will eventually decline into self-devaluation, self-criticism, and perhaps depression. Grandiosity which has failed to undergo maturation into positive self-esteem expects and demands absolute control of others and the environment. To ward off the potential ravages of an unrealistically harsh and demanding grandiose part of the self, a characterological defense is erected. That defense consists of reducing efforts to less than one's potential: for example, not investing oneself totally in an endeavor, not studying very much for a test, or in some ways leaving an escape hatch open. This escape hatch is constructed so that if there is failure it is defensively deemed to be due only to a lack of effort and not a lack of ability; thereby, one's grandiose self is maintained intact. On the other hand, if full efforts were expended and the wished-for responses were not forthcoming, the experience would be emotionally devastating. Additionally, if minimal efforts produce a good effect, this is a delectable experience, providing magical confirmation of power and brilliance. A similar cycle has been recognized among college students who do not study for exams: If an exam is failed it is due to lack of study and not ability; yet if the exam is passed without studying, it provides a confirmation of brilliance. If exam questions seem unsolvable, however, feelings of inadequacy result which paralyze thinking ability and insure a bad grade. The sense of self-esteem is further eroded, creating withdrawal from studying and even poorer grades.

The narcissistic individual characteristically experiences a sense of emptiness, lack of initiative, diffuse sensitivity and vulnerability to other people, intense ambitiousness, grandiose fantasies combined with a feeling of inferiority, and overdependence on external admiration and acclaim (1). The narcissistic personality is not primarily swayed by *guilt* but may become overwhelmed by *embarrassment* and *shame*, a reaction in part to the breakthrough to the grandiose self and the unneutralized exhibitionism which is part of that more primitive self. The nuclear problem in narcissistic disturbance is a defect in the internal structures which maintain self-esteem and self-cohesiveness (1). Other people ("selfobjects," a term indicating that others are experienced as an extension of or part of oneself, forming a functional unit) function as a substitute for the self-esteem regulating structures that the individual is unable to provide internally. People are often valued by the narcissist for their *function*, which is to maintain a sense of stability and a positive coloring to the individual's self-representation (3). Because external objects provide the regulation and confirmation of value and esteem, there is an overattachment to such objects, combined with a sense of exquisite vulnerability—as if one's emotional fate were in the hands of others.

The child's ongoing legitimate claim for approving attention, rather than being responded to, may be belittled and ridiculed at the very moment when she most proudly wants to display herself. The grandiosity and exhibitionism at the center of the developmental thrust in this phase is normal, and will hopefully be integrated to an appropriate sense of self-esteem and ambition. One has only to observe children aged three to six to see how the urge to display their budding mastery and talents, and to have an admiring response, is an integral part of interactions with important adults. If the adult response is nonrecognition, or, worse yet, shame and ridicule for being exhibitionistic, a pathological and unrelenting ambition may result. This pathological ambition, which is a driven need for approval, is one basis for the compulsions of "workaholics." The unrelenting ambition does not allow even remarkable successes to be enjoyed, just as the compulsive eater does not feel emotionally satiated after an elaborate meal. Coupled with pathological ambition and the polarity of grandiosity/self-depreciation is an ever-present fear of ridicule, rebuff, and shame.

One young woman described how a critical rebuff from her parents when she was a child would prompt a narcissistic injury and with it a sense of rage and shame. She would retreat to her room feeling defeated and empty; it was hours before she could venture out to try again. The parents, in imposing their own needs, did not recognize or respond to her needs. She felt that she had to be perfect to elicit a positive response from her parents; since this response was not forthcoming, the ideal of perfection which she felt she would have to attain was exalted still further: perhaps being even better and even more perfect would finally bring the desired loving confirmation. But this, too, was impossible to achieve, leaving her with a sense of profound inadequacy and ineptitude.

This pathology may also be produced by parents who emphasize the extraordinary talent and perfection of the child, and respond to each scribbling produced by the child as if it were a miracle and a masterpiece. There is a healthy sense of overvaluation which most parents have of their children's efforts, but an expectation of perfection and greatness with each effort is maladaptive and destructive of both parents and child. The child will experience disappointment and probably resentment when the rest of the world fails to corroborate the level of endowment and effort ascribed by the parents. The sense of perfection and mutual admiration existing in the family (more frequently in families with only children) often dooms the child, outside the home, to difficulty in completing projects which require sustained and practiced effort. The child at once begins to see how much *unpraised* work is necessary for the completion, and is unable to tolerate the disillusionment accompanying delayed or diminished positive response from others.

A narcissistic mother may create a profound sense of ineptitude accompanying fear and avoidance of self-assertion in her children. An aura of fragility surrounds the mother, so that self-expression in the child is equated with destructiveness. Such a situation is experienced by the child as tenuous, unpredictable, and inconsistent, so that the child has the conscious sense of "walking on eggshells" lest the mother fragment, become enraged, or withdraw.

Persons with narcissistic pathology have a sense of self alternating between the poles of grandiosity and deprecation. One series of studies (4) found that the mothers of children presenting with "pseudo-backwardness" (an internal inhibition of competent and successful strivings which would have been chronologically and intellectually possible) were uniformly characterized by a deficient sense of self-worth, regarding themselves as defective and inadequate as people and as mothers. *The mothers uniformly pictured their children in the same way.* The children seemingly shared these attributes and *complied with this percep-*

tion in order to preserve the maternal bond which they felt necessary. To maintain the bond of togetherness and harmony, the children defined themselves as the mother did, although it involved accepting attitudes and expectations which were deleterious and destructive.

Another family dynamic in which success later becomes an issue involves the child who experiences herself as a narcissistic focus for fulfillment of one or both parents. For example, a girl may play the role of gratifying her mother by becoming an extension of the mother's desires and feelings, and then fail to fulfill her own potential, including the establishment of separateness and individuality. The girl may then need to take an extreme position of rebellion or revenge in order to establish her distinctness. Learning disabilities in some children are motivated by this type of rebellion (5). Some women with narcissistic pathology focus on what has been metaphorically described as penis envy: a concrete depiction of the conviction that some essential feature necessary for vitality and success is missing. This conviction of something being missing may also focus on the brain, with the belief that men have a certain type of intelligence or intellectual assertion which women lack. For these women, success seems available only through deviousness and manipulation, using sexual charms or other feminine wiles which utilize their "weakness." There may be a strong sense of injury or deprivation, with insistence upon redress of their grievances (6). Hostility toward men often accompanies this insistence upon redress of grievances, with alteration of envy and contempt for the man luxuriating in perceived privileges. The privileges and pleasures which are afforded men, and the development of achievement in men, are perceived as unattainable by the female. When women in this group do achieve great success, they often have nagging doubts about their capacity, resulting in the belief that they have fooled people and gained their success in a fraudulent manner.

An alternate source of pathology is the mother whose needs and perceptions become so entwined with the child that no sense of separateness or distinctness develops; the child's needs are seen only in relationship to the mother's own needs. This also disallows the growth of an autonomous and relevant self-image. The child developing under these circumstances must remain oriented consistently toward the mother. Seeking guidance, direction, and initiative solely from others, such a child devalues and disregards her own internal signals, perceptions, and creativity, with resultant diminished self-esteem. These developmental events manifest clinically in mirroring and idealizing transference phenomena in treatment in the constellation of a narcissistic character. The transmission of affective tone in the caregiving environment has a significant influence on later development. The happy, talking, singing mother has a smiling, gurgling baby in its crib. The mother who is anxious and tense has a fussy and vomiting baby, while an angry mother has a crying and negativistic baby (7).

For the narcissistic individual, there is insufficient internal regulation of self-esteem. A pathological degree of grandiosity and perfection-striving makes certain events threatening or intolerable. For example, for some individuals a structured learning environment, such as college, represents a self-confirming process, with school and professors serving the function of maintaining feedback, regulation, and structure. The threat of losing the maintenance of this self-confirming process upon graduation may be intolerable. The concomitant loss of self-esteem, or more severely, actual fragmentation of the sense of self, at the time of graduation is an indicant of this pathology (8). Any sense of failure is experienced as a personal tragedy for the narcissistically vulnerable individual.

For the narcissistic woman, excessive grandiosity and ambition must be concealed. Praise at work or the public recognition of an accomplishment may paradoxically make her depressed, and she may also act to undermine her accomplishment in some fashion. The response of depression may result from a sense of fragmentation and an experience of depletion. The accompaniment of an accomplishment is a fear of isolation and emptiness, as if the nurturance and gratification of others would be withdrawn if she were not constantly in need. The illusion of being haunted by a "dark side" can persist in the woman's mind until confronted and explored therapeutically.

Narcissistic conflicts result in an exquisite sensitivity to, and excessive focus on, the self. There is a great preoccupation with how one is viewed in the eyes of others, and an inordinate concern about the risk of making mistakes and being a failure. Narcissistic people will avoid situations which are unpredictable in order to insure engagement only in successful activities. Especially high ambitions and expectations, often unrealistic, alternate with low self-respect, fear of failure, and ready self-reproach and self-criticism for failing to live up to expectations. These people generally pursue endeavors only to a point, losing interest before the moment of actual testing. Applications for jobs or submissions of projects to be evaluated may be withdrawn at the final moment, or steady pursuit of a goal abandoned at a final step, often concomitant with a sudden disavowal of interest in what had been previously a highly invested endeavor.

People with narcissistic pathology pursue endeavors which result in admiration and enhancement of their *perceived* esteem, as opposed to those which involve intrinsic desire for accomplishment, desire of the activities necessary to such accomplishment, or desire of the goals being sought. These individuals have a sense of entitlement in which rewards are expected to flow flawlessly and without interruption. Noncompliance or opposition by another person, involving a failure to respond as an extension of the wishes and desires of the narcissistic individual, may result in a narcissistic rage. The narcissistic person is then easily dissuaded from an endeavor by the perception that others do not share the same sense of entitlement which she experiences. She may, for example, be able to work successfully until she senses that not everyone feels she is perfect, the best, or the brightest, and then she may suddenly lose interest and stop.

This type of woman may adapt to narcissistic problems by a close involvement with an admired man who is successful and in whose shadow she feels complete. By a kind of fusion with him she shares in the qualities which are attributed to him and his possessions: physical, material, and emotional. But she pays a high emotional price for such a resigned adaptation, since the self-esteem is not the result of her own endeavors. Her resentment of perceived deprivation and personal defect must be repressed in order to maintain the bond which is the source of her narcissistic satisfaction. Disillusionment and crisis occur at times of separation or divorce, or even at times when the overvalued and idealized man seems to (surprisingly, for her) have difficulties and uncertainties himself.

Competent work function is perceived by some narcissistic women as a *role* that one plays, similar to a stage performance.

Seeing competent function as a role disavows it as one's own. An extreme example is the individual who feels "I don't know who *me* is without the role." Not all narcissistic disturbances will result in inhibition or even compromise of work. Some individuals are able, through their skill and talent, to effect a situation in which reality does indeed conform to and confirm a sense of omnipotence. For these people, the external rewards are great. Disturbances in narcissism can provide great stimuli in the motivation for success, and the opposite of work inhibition is work compulsion. (See Chapter 11.)

In summary, as an adult, the narcissistic woman will sense being "fake" and will feel empty. She will need others to validate her own ideas and feelings, and ultimately and most pathologically, to confirm her identity and existence. The woman who does not experience herself as a separate person—who feels she is nothing without a man, her job, or some other significant source of validation and confirmation—experiences a devitalized self without a sense of goals, competence, or direction, and needs constant mirroring approval from others. When self-esteem is contingent on the approval of others to some degree, behavior is guided more predominately by fear of rejection or loss of love.

CHAPTER 5

Sexual Identity: Formation and Elaboration

SEXUAL IDENTITY IS the predominant step in the psychosexual line of development between the ages of two and five years. Sexual identity has many aspects, and includes exposure to parental and cultural views of behaviors, attitudes, and coping which are considered masculine or feminine. Sexual-role identity, then, is fashioned by an amalgamation of internal and external elements of masculinity or femininity (1). The phases in development of sexual identity include morphological (anatomical and hormonal) identity, gender identity (established by eighteen to twenty-four months of age,) and sexual-role identity, including the distinctions of masculinity or femininity.

The girl's self-image is built early upon a biologically based femininity facilitated by parental mirroring responses. These initiating elements lead to a variety of identifications with gender traits of her mother, and secondarily her father. These responses will be shaped and molded by the child's basic desire to please and be loved by each parent. Both parents foster and orient the feminine individuation of their daughter. This provides a basic feminine identity, body image, and sense of self.

A mother who is secure in her own sense of femininity and self-worth serves as an identification figure and as an affirmative mirror for her daughter's own unique ways of expressing emerging femininity. In continuing response to her developmental needs the little girl actively turns to the father for a number of reasons, including the wish for affirmation as well as a jealous wish to possess the father. This becomes most apparent at ages four and five, and it is particularly important that she perceive her mother's delight, affirmation, and empathic mirroring response in so doing. She can be traumatized at this time either by the absence of such a response from the mother or by a response which reveals the mother's sense of jealousy and rivalry. A positive and loving response may not always be easy for the mother, as the daughter's special attention to and by the father may stir unsettled questions about the mother's own value and femininity; a jealous and competitive counterreaction may be provoked by the daughter's competitiveness. The daughter's integration and sublimation of both parental models are best effected by parental encouragement of age-appropriate recognitions, affects, and behaviors.

The mother, in taking on life vitally and energetically, provides the model of what a competent and assertive woman is and does—a model with whom the daughter will identify as a step in seeing herself become successful. The daughter needs to experience both parents empathically mirroring her own idealization and sense of grandness about herself in order to utilize these as ideals and ambitions, respectively. Both parents meet needs for affirmation and validation from their positions as important idealized persons who make themselves available for identification. The phase-appropriate reflection by the parents of emerging aspects of self-expression, sexuality, expansiveness, grandiosity, and idealization allows the emerging self to incorporate the healthy aspects of all these qualities.

The relationship of the parents with each other is important as well. The model of a woman, the model of a man whom she loves, and the model of a marriage are all offered within the original family. The accretion of these early experiences will later manifest as expectations and attitudes in both work and love.

Many things can upset the normal course of a girl progressing toward confident womanhood. The death of a parent, for example, may produce an impact on self-esteem and relationships with other people, especially those of the lost parent's gender (2). If the girl loses an ongoing relationship with either parent through separation or divorce, evolving sexual identity may be affected. In losing her father, she may feel unloved, abandoned, unattractive, and unable to hold the first man she loves, establishing a precedent for those who follow. The loss of her mother deletes the ongoing contact and identification, including the impact on evolving sexual identity. The nature and degree of impact also depends upon the age at which the child suffers the loss (3). This developmental line may also be disrupted traumatically by such circumstances as parents' severe and incapacitating illnesses, physical disabilities, or extreme physical defects—to name only some of the situations which may be perceived by the child as diminishing her own desirability and lovableness.

A persistent question for the child is, "How do I get and retain my parents' love and respect?" The answer is fashioned from the wish to conform to an image which will achieve that love and respect: i.e., the wish to do what will create the most favorable possibility of a positive response. The parents' conscious and unconscious needs and attitudes are thus reflected in the child. It is said that "the unconscious of the parent becomes the conscious of the child" in this process. Heinrich Pestalozzi (reputedly) put it another way: "You can drive the devil out of your garden but you will find him again in the garden of your son." If helplessness and vulnerability are reinforced by means of the invisible chains the mother experiences from her own childhood, it becomes especially difficult for her daughter to not experience the same invisible chains.

The mother may provide mixed messages about becoming a woman. Despite the ambiguity and confusion of these messages, the daughter must introject and integrate them into her self-concept. She may experience guilt, anxiety, and a sense of lonely alienation if she challenges one of the prescribed roles.

Women have often been stereotypically regarded in psychoanalytic theory as inherently masochistic. This view is supported by the observations that they are usually less strong physically than men; that intercourse involves being penetrated; that menstruation, defloration, and childbirth involve both pain and blood; and that society encourages women to inhibit their assertiveness and aggressiveness. However, there is nothing innately or motivationally masochistic in any of these characteristics. Just as masochism as a motivating force or underlying dynamic could mistakenly be postulated and given "confirmatory validation" by the above-cited painful experiences of femaleness, so, in a similarly paralogical way, a woman can find validation of her assumption that being aggressive will result in loss of love when she expresses anger and finds that indeed a loved one withdraws.

A mother who has difficulty dealing with aggression directly and deflects it with a facade of passivity and overindulgent helpfulness will tolerate only these mechanisms in her daughter. The daughter's aggression is acceptable only if it is expressed as a reaction-formation. She can cry if she is angry, but she cannot raise her voice or otherwise act assertively. There is a double thrust in this process: a molding and shaping by the mother through her own verbalization and responses, and a modeling and identification by the daughter. For a mother of this type, such complementarity is always necessary; there has to be reciprocity or compliance in every encounter. The daughter must conform to expected behavior in order to live in harmony with the mother. Daughters who have resisted this kind of maternal molding often seem troublesome as children but ultimately make a healthier adaptation.

Questions about the effect on early childhood development of families in which both parents work outside the home await further study. An empathic responsive matrix is necessary for psychological growth, but does it make a difference whether the child's biological mother is the provider of this matrix? Does it make a difference whether one or several people are involved in mothering?

Kohut (4) emphasizes: "One must think not simply in terms of 'mothering' and 'mother,' but in terms of the total complexity of an environment and whether it is positive or negative." The wish of a healthy woman to have a baby may represent a psychological manifestation of her most important ambitions and ideals, a sort of culmination of her self-expression. On the other hand, the wish for a baby can be an attempt to cure a psychological disturbance, motivated by a vaguely conscious sense that the baby can consolidate a fragmented self and provide feelings of sufficiency and value.

Kohut (5) writes:

Now, I do not see, at least from my own clinical experience, that the narcissistic injury that undoubtedly is connected with the absence of the visible genital in little girls is, in essence, different from the narcissistic injury to the little boy who discovers that his penis is very small as compared with the penis of a grown man. I believe, however, that a child is much more significantly influenced by the empathic attitude of the grownups around him or her than by the givens of organic equipment. A mother's and father's admiration of the little girl as a little girl, in her sweetness, in her future bearing of children, in whatever potentials of her femininity she displays will provide her ultimately when she becomes a woman with the same degree of security and idealizability that the man has if *he* was accepted by his admiring and happy and glad parents when he was a little boy, even though his penis was small. The importance of the matrix of empathy in which we grow up cannot be overestimated. (pp. 776–777)

Some important knowledge of the emerging sexual identity of children has come out of direct observational work with normal children. Frankel and Sherrick (6) observed that in a group of toddlers, aged two to three years, boys and girls reacted to each other without regard to sexual preference and selected activities without regard to whether they were traditionally masculine or feminine; boys and girls of this age group played equally readily with dolls and kitchen utensils, trucks and tractors.

Male and female psychological differentiation has been established by direct observation of infants and children to occur by approximately eighteen months of age (7, 8). The direct observational data indicate that genital awareness is evident between sixteen and nineteen months of age. This genital phase is characterized by behavior indicating underlying genital arousal, such as frequent and intense manipulation, as well as marked curiosity regarding the genitals of others. This early genital phase would be obviously free of Oedipal resonance, but is closely connected with the parallel development at this time of consolidation of self and object representations, including those of the genital area. The findings indicated that discovery of the genital distinction is usually low-keyed. The children for whom marked upset or anxiety accompanies the discovery of genital distinction have sustained, during their first year of life, a physical trauma such as surgery or serious illness, or suffered a disturbance in the mother-child relationship, such as an actual prolonged separation or an emotional distancing of the sort which would accompany, for example, a mother's postpartum depression. Reactions include sleep disturbance, bowel and bladder function disturbance, negativism, increased dependence on the mother, and animal phobias (with particular fear of being bitten by animals). Boys fear that their penis will be lost; girls question why a penis does not exist. An important aspect of these early reactions is linked to primitive ego organization and a fear of object loss and loss of a sense of self. These reactions are unlike the reactions termed "castration reactions" in the actual Oedipal phase. These observations lend further support to the idea that "castration anxiety" in boys and "penis envy" in girls are the result of particular developmental disturbances rather than normal aspects of negotiation.

Frankel and Sherrick also observed the emergence of sexual identity as reflected in children's play. Among children 4.6 to 5 years of age, domestic play for girls became more sophisticated. The children had become more independent, managing play families and communicating about matters of a domestic nature. Girls were observed to emulate progressively their mother's gender role behavior in their play. They were observed to have "an impressive sense of common purpose as females." Such play at mothering and at emulating the roles of their mothers validates and consolidates both maternal and feminine identification.

The observations of Frankel and Sherrick (6) indicated that preschool girls felt slightly more secure than boys and were more sophisticated and creative in their play. The postulation of this occurrence was in partial relationship to a somewhat advanced cognitive level with a lower constitutional activity level. Thus this facet of the explanation would involve biological inclinations of girls versus boys. Additionally, it was postulated that a somewhat greater sense of confidence resulted from the girl being the same sex as the mother, and, even in the nursery school situation, from being the same sex as the teacher. The girl's initial advantage is later modified, however. The boy's disadvantages of being sexually opposite to the mother and displaying a level of physical activity which could strain the new mother's empathy ultimately become his means to replace his primary caretaker (Mother) during the second and third years of life and obtain a sense of maleness by identification with his father. Frankel and Sherrick observed that the girls aged 4.6 to 5 years were more comfortable associating with other girls in their play group, and would exclude boys or use them as "extras." This attitude took on a "rather militant quality at about the time when behavior presumably indicative of the envy of males appears." They noted that "this exclusion seems partly to serve a defensive function by giving the girls a compensatory feeling of strength and status, as well as the strong sense of 'sisterhood' being a growth-promoting aspect for consolidation of their femaleness and femininity."

By contrast, groups seem to play a much less significant role in the consolidation of sexual identity for boys. Additionally, competitiveness seems much less sublimated among boys, and thereby more disruptive to their endeavors at mutual play. A similar phenomenology is commonly observed among adult males, who are normally less intimate and less reliant on a cohesive community of friends and close associates. The precise linkages between an individual's manifest behavior, conscious thought, internal attitudes, and unconscious motivations are identifiable only by analytic exploration, and these observations are therefore simply generic.

There is evidence from observational studies (9) that the girl's desire to have a baby is an expression of identification with the mother. It is evident from these studies that girls who do not have a positive and loving relationship with their mothers do not have the wish to have a baby. Their play, likewise, does not include mimicking of mothering activities.

Erikson (10) observed imaginative themes and special configurations in the play of children. Although gender distinctions were not an initial focus of his study, he made important observations about the differing concept of inner space among boys and girls. He noted a "female" configuration in the construction of play objects by girls: The most common was an enclosure (a space defined by a boundary structured by the girl, e.g., a circle made by blocks), with the focus on the interior, such as walls to represent a house, with attention directed toward the arrangement of furniture *inside*. People, animals, and important events were inside this interior or enclosure. There would be an occasional elaborate doorway for entry to this inner space. In a number of cases the interior was intruded upon by animals or by dangerous men. For boys, the scenes constructed from the same material were *protrusions* such as cylinders, cones, and high towers. Almost all the scenes constructed by the boys were *exterior* scenes or outside enclosures, with all the activity occurring outside the structure. There was much focus upon automobile accidents and the danger of collapse or downfall of the high structures and towers.

The predominantly recurrent theme of the boys was of structures achieving height, then toppling down, usually accompanied by violent motion. The recurrent theme of the girls was of interior space and of occurrences or action which opened or enclosed this space. Erikson concluded that particular construction play and use of space paralleled the morphology of the genitalia (10).

These research findings by Erikson parallel the analytic findings that structural representations as symbols are highly cathected by preadolescent fantasy and preoccupation. In addition to symbolic significance, the interpretation may be seen as somatic, with the prevalence of interest by boys in action-oriented, aggressive, and outdoor activities, and the girl's interests appearing to be consistent with her "social assignment" to the indoors of houses and love for family and children. The children studied by Erikson were aged ten to twelve.

Most of the original theories of psychoanalysis concerning womanhood are based on the theory of "genital trauma," i.e., the supposed recognition by the little girl that she does not possess a penis. This organ is then envied, according to theory, with the girl turning from the mother, who is depreciated because she did not adequately endow her, to the father, who has not been cheated like the mother and will presumably not cheat the girl. The little girl unconsciously expects that her father will give her a baby, which will be a substitute for the penis. The final step for the woman in this theory is to relinquish aggressiveness, which is associated with the male, and adopt a "passive-masochistic" orientation. The supposed confirmatory data for this theory are found in its consistent demonstration among female patients in psychoanalysis.

It is not the raw data but the inferences and conclusions drawn from it, and thus the ultimate theoretical implications, which are suspect. An alternate explanation and synthesis could be illustrated by summarizing some of the pertinent information from a patient who presented an abundance of this type of material and whose conflict centered in this area. The appearance of this type of material, rather than validating a constellation of psychic progression for all or even most women, represents a particular type of pathological development for some women. Such a case vignette appears in the next chapter.

For prepubertal girls, the wish to have a baby is a complex issue, but is deeply rooted in an identification with the mother. The mother often facilitates this process by encouraging the girl to imitate her maternity: the child's own "baby" is a doll. Any woman who chooses not to have a baby and be a mother must *disidentify* with her own mother in this important way. If there were early aspects of deprivation or conflict in this relationship between mother and daughter, there will be a wish to disidentify, and in some cases to push away, to be as different from the mother as possible. There may be a turning toward the father for care and attention, which would eroticize otherwise basic nurturing, caring, and maternal functions, thus complicating the issue.

Part of this early observation of the mother with whom she is to identify involves some frightening aspects for the small girl. The observation and conceptualization of menstruation, pregnancy, and other bodily functions, interpreted with the literal reasoning of the small child, is often traumatic. The curiosity of anticipating having a baby and being a mother is at best ambivalent. There is associated blood, pain, and violation of one's own body.

The mother's intrusion of her own feelings, as well as the mother's comfort about her own sexuality, provide the backdrop for certain aspects of development. She may communicate the attitude that the little girl's genitals are dirty and not to be touched or explored.

Issues of mastery and control for the girl, especially sphincter management, are difficult. Women involved in sports, athletics, camping, and other outdoor activities may find it relatively more difficult than men to attend to bodily functions, particularly if they have menstrual periods during these times. The menses are spontaneous and there is no sphincter control involved. The girl may then also view menses as something dirty and undesirable.

In clinical work we must carefully distinguish between interventions and interpretations which have an *organizing* but not a *therapeutic* effect. For example, the interpretation of "penis envy" in women is this kind of problem because it can serve as a metaphor, as Roiphe and Galenson (7) suggest, for such otherwise ill-defined free-floating conflicts as feelings of worthlessness, inadequacy, deprivation, damage, or a general sense of envy. Metaphors such as this may be concretely enshrined as developmental milestones rather than reflections of a need to organize and label pathological manifestations of development.

Some aspects of psychoanalytic theory collude with social preconceptions, albeit from a different vantage point. Much previous analytic literature contains subtle hints that it is other than a natural course of development for women to seek careers—a pursuit which has been attributed to "too strong an identification with the father" or even "pathological penis envy" (11). The search for achievement and success has been labeled as a "misplaced masculine striving."

The girl has to contend with obvious anatomical differences from boys. She becomes the loser in the urinary-jet competition with her brother, since her sensations are not as localized and there is not an external organ upon which to focus physical manipulation. Her organs, being internal, belong to the realm of future hope: breasts and perhaps babies forthcoming. Cognitive development does not allow the girl to make abstract projections into the future (nor is this possible for the boy, who compares himself to his father and finds himself quite little). The girl will nevertheless wish intensely that she had what the boy has—but only if something in her life is *empathically* missing: if one or both parents love a boy more, or fail to impart to her a loving sense of security. There may be envy of the boy's position, activities, and scope. A girl who envies a boy does not wish to *become* a boy; she wishes to be who she is but to have the privileges, entitlements, and narcissistic and social advantages that the boy enjoys.

It is sometimes very difficult for the three- or four-year-old girl to understand, especially if her parents are insensitive to her developmental needs, that none of her interpretations and concrete reasoning concerning different anatomical configurations are true. If the young girl sees that a boy and a man enjoy aspects of freedom, autonomy, and privilege which she does not have, she may identify this deprivation as specifically linked to the only observable difference: anatomical construction. Circumstances which may arouse envy are the birth of a new sibling, with consequent redirection of attention to the infant, or the mother's overvaluation of another sibling.

Masochism and penis envy are signals of internal conflict for the male as well as the female. Normal penis envy is found in a very small boy who sees a big and admired father whose total anatomy and power are concretely symbolized in the mature genitalia. Males who have particular developmental problems in this area, the most prominent of these being obligatory homosexuality, have a pathological penis envy. This envy manifests in the compulsive search for a man with a large phallus. The neurotic wish is to incorporate or "take in" the magic phallus and thus become endowed with the power, potency, and esteem which are deemed missing.

How is it that power, strength, integrity, and even creativity are, on different levels, all symbolized by the male sex organ? In pre-Oedipal development, the mother is seen by the child as a powerful, active, and omnipotent person to whom the child must submit. The passage from passivity toward activity is achieved during this developmental period by an identification with the mother's activity (12). During this period, the mother seems capable of everything to the girl and seems to possess every ideal attribute. But if the girl has a domineering mother, she may continue to experience submission, powerlessness, and helplessness. In this case, viewing the mother as "castrated" may be a defense resulting from a desire to be free of her overwhelming domination. Thus, alliance with the father represents emancipation.

For both the male and female the penis is thus connected with many primitive ideas about power. Penis envy can be seen as a defensive maneuver caused by the desire to free oneself from pathological maternal domination, and not as the desire of the daughter to acquire a penis.

Corresponding in some sense to penis envy is the boy's fear of losing or damaging such an exposed and vulnerable organ. There is also, in addition to real and imagined differences in a boy and girl, very possibly deep and pervasive envy of the woman's capacity to produce other human beings. Only the girl can become a mother. This envy appears to be most consciously accessible in males who have the strongest feminine identification—most profoundly so in transsexual men.

Male developmental difficulties are different in some important ways from those of the female. The boy must give up a primary nurturing figure in order to identify with the same-sexed parent, his father. The girl does not have to relinquish her primary nurturing figure in order to form the deep bonds of identification with a same-sexed parent. An inherent problem for the girl is that her identification with the parent of her own sex involves a dependent and regressive pull and makes autonomy a somewhat more difficult issue.

If penis envy occurs as a manifest phenomenon, it is already a sign, as stated earlier, that something has gone wrong in the girl's development; sexual identity issues or a narcissistic wound may be involved. Penis envy is thus a pathological rather than an expectable and normal stage building block in a woman's sexual development.

The belief that the girl perceives herself as a male with missing parts is contradicted by evidence of fundamental stability of gender and sexual identity in both sexes (13). Most recent direct observational studies of normal children support the findings of Edgecumbe (14) that "concerning the phallic phase itself: rather than postulating that recognition of her lack of a penis forces the girl to abandon a masculine position for a feminine one, we suggest the less biased view that awareness of the significance of physical sexual differences between boys and girls and between children and adults aids both boys and girls in consolidating their sexual identity."

The identification process uses as primary models both the mother and the father. To a lesser extent siblings and surrogate parents, such as teachers and a variety of significant others, also serve as models to be imitated. These other models can become more important if there is some emotional disruption or other unavailability in the family unit. For example, when a parent is lost by divorce or death, or is unavailable emotionally, surrogate parent figures gain greater importance. In the most comfortable situation, the girl identifies primarily with her mother. If this process is disrupted, there is a price to pay: a feeling of insecurity and conflict about herself as a girl and later as a woman. Other than overt loss or disruption in the early mother-daughter relationship (such as prolonged emotional or physical illness), if the mother herself is insecure and uncertain about herself, this becomes part of the introject of the daughter. Identification is with both the unconscious contents of the mother (sense of self, unresolved conflicts, etc.) and the conscious contents (coping style, behavior, defense mechanisms, etc.).

It is interesting to note parenthetically that only within very recent times have there been any female superheroes with whom the young girl can identify. Until the advent of Wonder Woman and the Bionic Woman there were no socially accepted popular fantasy figures possessed of omnipotent powers who were females. This did not limit, however, the personal creation of private fantasies of omnipotent female figures in the minds of women.

The girl is openly proud of, and prized for, traits akin to those of her mother. She proudly displays mothering tendencies toward dolls and is applauded for other acts which openly reproduce those of her mother. In families where the father is aloof and withholds emotionally, the girl may exaggerate these characteristics to win him over, hoping to elicit the kind of response from him that she fantasizes him as giving to her mother. These actions on the girl's part may become openly flirtatious and seductive in their caricature of adultness. Another type of father, who needs this sort of response because of his own inadequacies, may openly solicit such displays from his young daughter. The response of a psychologically mature father to his daughter's sexuality and to her entire personality can help her negotiate her own ambivalence about growing up and the new sensations, fantasies, and responsibilities she is experiencing. If she grows up in an atmosphere in which she is valued by both her mother and her father, and sees her mother as valued in all respects by her father, she will not feel then or later as if she is "missing something" physically or emotionally.

CHAPTER 6

Oedipal Issues:
The Taboo of Success

THE OEDIPAL SITUATION involves the daughter's fear of angry abandonment by the mother should she succeed in winning exclusively the attention and love of her father. Such a success for the girl would invoke the unconscious equation of this success with vanquishment of the Oedipal rival and its associated sense of guilt and fear of retaliation or abandonment, culminating in a protective, self-imposed defeat. This dangerous success is impeded or prevented, thus attenuating the perceived threat of goal attainment. Under certain conditions, this series of psychological events can become pathological and success at winning the father's exclusive love is unconsciously generalized to other successes or completions such as vocational or work performance. This mechanism may become one of the reasons for the need to impose defeat on oneself. Success at a later age would be perceived unconsciously as retaliation against the mother, linked developmentally with earlier rivalries between the child and parent.

The vicissitudes of the Oedipal conflict can manifest in work inhibition in both children and adults. The family situation may intensify a girl's fear of angry, rejecting abandonment by the mother or of simply a failure of support and assurance for important developmental needs of achievement and mastery. This can create an impetus to avoid successful competition with the mother. A passive retreat occurs, with the failure of application of the girl's full potential in competent endeavors. The sphere of competence in endeavors which should widen as she develops biologically and psychologically is thwarted by her failure to apply herself fully.

Since everyone goes through Oedipal development, why doesn't everyone have a success phobia? Several patterns have emerged, alone or in concert, which can create a pathological resolution to normal Oedipal issues. Certain psychopathology manifesting as performance inhibition or "success phobia" has been causally linked with Oedipal conflict.

Oedipal conflict can be intensified in several ways. Physical intimidation or abuse from a parent or sibling may reinforce an unconscious equation between assertiveness, on one hand, and aggression, violence, or abandonment, on the other. The desire in the small child to surpass a powerful rival generates both guilt and fear of equally violent retaliation, resulting in the inhibition or withholding of aggression. This inhibition of aggression is then extended in application to assertion in general. The phobic extension of this conflict is inhibition of assertion, which may apply to vocational or professional assertion.

Oedipal fears can be compounded when alienation between parents is so extreme that a child can easily win the parent of the opposite sex away from the other parent. Examples of this kind of situation include the loss of a parent by separation, divorce, or death, the psychological absence of a parent, excessive parental narcissism, or excessive seductive closeness of a parent to an opposite-sexed child. For example, an ambitious father may subtly depreciate his wife's endeavors to his daughter in the hopes that his daughter will make up for this failing. This exchange becomes intensified if the daughter actually does surpass the mother in some important respect, such as obtaining a professional or college degree when the mother has none. As a result, the daughter may feel excessively guilty and fear abandonment by the mother. The daughter may unconsciously identify failing before the final step toward success with a position of passivity and safety from retribution, retaliation, or angry abandonment. Thus, the final step or passageway into successful completion of a task entailing promotion, graduation, marriage, or the like is manifested by anxiety, creating an inhibition of effort and the fear of retaliation or abandonment.

One woman in the final months of nursing school began to have increasing difficulty concentrating and studying, and became anxious during examinations. She considered stopping school and abandoning her career plans. She mentioned the similar position her mother had been in a number of years ago when the mother became pregnant and had to drop out of nursing school, also with only a few months remaining. This woman unconsciously equated completing nursing school with a direct affront to her mother; she would have been eclipsing her mother on common turf.

In considering the contribution to development made by the Oedipal phase, Erikson discussed the polar positions of "initiative versus guilt" during this stage:

> The danger of this stage is a sense of guilt over the goals contemplated and the acts initiated in one's exuberant enjoyment of new locomotor and mental power: acts of aggressive manipulation and coercion which soon go far beyond the executive capacity of organism and mind and therefore call for an energetic halt to one's contemplated initiative. While autonomy concentrates on keeping potential rivals out, and therefore can lead to jealous rage often directed against encroachments by younger siblings, initiative brings with it anticipatory rivalry with those who have been there first and may, therefore, occupy with their superior equipment the field toward which one's initiative is directed. Infantile jealousy and rivalry, those often embittered and yet essentially futile attempts at demarcating a sphere of unquestioned privilege, now come to a climax in a final contest for a favored position with the [father]. The usual failure leads to resignation, guilt, and anxiety. (1, pp. 255–256).

When these ghosts from the past persist in adult life and create a continuation of internal conflict around rivalry, initiative, and assertion, the competition to be the "best and favorite" may lead to inhibited aggression, with anxiety and guilt over self-assertion manifested in one's work and career.

A type of pathological effort to repair developmental difficulties in the Oedipal period is illustrated by the following patient.

CASE STUDY: THE DOCTOR'S SHADOW

Margaret, age thirty-three, came to treatment in a state of despairing depression, stating that she felt like she was not her own person, but the shadow of her husband, a prominent physician. She described how her frustration and anguish conflicted with her fear of stepping away from this dependent position; she was aware of her gratification in her current role as well as her fear of failing should she attempt greater independence.

She stated her frustration most poignantly. "I really can't feel free, can't release myself. I know I have a lot of potential and talent but I've never really allowed myself to use it. My whole life actually centers around my husband, being the perfect physician's wife, and having everything I do in that role be approved of. It's as if I can't do anything without his approval. I enjoy the praise I get for such wifely things as preparing perfect meals and being a gracious and beautiful hostess. He is security for me. He is a man showing emotion toward me, and he knows what he wants out of life." She further elaborated on her depressions and the constant feeling that something vital and important in her life was missing, which she "could not quite put a finger on."

In analysis she initially wanted to be led and directed, and was uncomfortable with the process of saying anything and everything that came to mind, of looking inward and generating her own associations. She described how she carefully avoided certain areas of responsibility, such as giving talks in public or assuming leadership roles in her community.

Her strong identification with her mother became apparent. This staunch and continuing bond included sharing the mother's interests and pursuits. She noted that she could only do well in areas in which her mother had done well, but that she didn't do *quite* as well as her mother. Her mother had completed her college degree, but Margaret had only completed three and a half years of college, not quite finishing her final semester. She was very careful not to affront her mother with raw competitiveness. When she prepared meals, or when she dressed for a major outing, there was always something missing, something not quite complete. She elaborated on how she could not perform at her total best; something always got in her way. She added, "I never could complete anything, I always leave one thing undone. I never really do anything quite as well as I can. I guess it's an insecure feeling. If I look nice and am completely dressed (which I never am) and sound bright, I laugh at myself, or make some stupid remark to put myself down. If I feel really attractive, I might dress in some cruddy way.''

Being valued seemed to create guilt as if such praise were undeserved. Margaret therefore sabotaged her efforts in some manner. Saying something stupid, appearing slightly askew, or leaving something undone were her disavowels of completeness and success.

As a very small girl she had witnessed her mother being subservient and deferential to her father, who was also a physician. Her brother seemed to have a favorite position with the man whose attention she sought, her father; the father chose her brother to work closely with him while she was assigned to household tasks. The brother was taken to the hospital to go on rounds with the father, but she was not. The father gave priority to his son even in small matters such as allowing the son more playtime with him. In analysis, Margaret acknowledged, for the first time, anger and frustration concerning the father who acted prejudicially and the mother who seemed not to regard herself or her daughter as important and vital. Margaret unconsciously despised her brother, yet cloaked this anger with the same ingratiating shroud her mother used. She continued to ask herself the despairing question, ''Why can't I be free and independent like other women?'' The answer was not obvious to her at the time because it lay buried beneath the blanket of her unconscious.

The only concrete difference she had been able to discern between her brother and herself at the age of five, she noted, was anatomical; therefore, the presence (or for her, she reasoned, the absence) of this seemingly important anatomical structure became the concretized explanation for the privileged status and deferential treatment her brother was accorded daily by both her mother and her father. This apparently magical organ made the brother like the father, and both were accorded respect and a sense of entitlement. Her envy and contempt could become focused, just as her brother's urinary streams could, as he proudly taunted her in saying that he could go to the bathroom off the back porch and she could not.

Early in adolescence, realizing that she could not receive the kind of love and respect from her father that she wished, she turned to other men in a promiscuous effort to repair her self-image, and to express revengefully the hostility engendered by a lack of appropriate and deserved responsiveness from her father. While being quite liberal and active in her sexual endeavors, she was careful to conceal these activities from her parents. She saw every man who pursued her as exciting, but they were all the same: they were all essentially equal in that they only wanted sex. Such dehumanization, a motive force in certain kinds of promiscuity, consciously equates every man and unconsciously gratifies the wish to be liked and loved by Father. If Father's desired love and esteem are not forthcoming, the unconscious reasons, then any other man will suffice, since all men are the same. Margaret's revenge, the other side of her wish to be positively responded to, took the form of dehumanizing many men. The men were "all the same" in that "all they wanted was sex." Thus they, like her father, were afraid of intimacy and emotional depth. She was, of course, unconsciously selecting only those men who would meet these expectations and who would not depart from this stereotypic view.

The full force of her repressed feelings and self-perception evolved in treatment and came to discovery largely through her transference perceptions of the analyst. These distortions of, and assumptions about, her self-image, and the intensity of her conscious and unconscious affect toward men particularly (but also women), could now be experienced, understood, and resolved in a definitive manner. The following dream will illustrate some aspects of this process. "I walked into your office for an appointment and suddenly realized that I was nude. I immediately felt good, that I was free, but I also felt very embarrassed and wanted to cover up. You began laughing at me and teasing me and telling me that I had better cover up. You also pointed out that one of my fingers was missing and that I was walking as if I were retarded. I then went around your office to look for some jewelry to put on—something of value, particularly gold." Her associations were of feeling retarded, perceiving herself to be less than adequate, and looking for something of value outside herself. She had begun to see the analyst as the father-brother who was ridiculing and teasing her, pointing out that she lacked something, now a finger, and earlier a penis, which her brother had mercilessly taunted her about. She remembered feeling laughed at and ridiculed by her brother for her naked body. Looking for valuable jewelry to hang on her, she realized, was her concretized reaction to the differences she perceived in their bodies. This difference in bodies—that her brother possessed something she did not—had become the only plausible explanation for the differences in treatment of herself and her brother. She elaborated on the paradoxical situation of knowing that she was bright, as opposed to retarded, yet assuming that her value lay in some external trapping, such as gold jewelry, or a successful husband, in whose shadow she was living.

Her further associations concerned the ways in which she was able to do her best totally only when she was doing things her mother didn't do. Something had always gotten in the way of achieving other goals. She recognized that significant factors in sabotaging successful endeavors of her own were fears of surpassing her mother, of being exposed as insignificant and incapable, and of feeling alone and devalued. The aggressiveness inherent in achievement had become restricted, as if it were the exclusive domain of the male, as had been demonstrated countless times with her father and brother. She had previously allowed herself to do only "womanly" things such as household tasks and pursuing a college degree in teaching. Even having an orgasm was restricted and inhibited to a large degree, since the frightening prospect of "letting go" with a man would mean letting go of her repressed aggression and sexuality.

She was able, during psychoanalysis, to complete her college degree and engage in a course of study for a doctorate. In a letter she wrote after her treatment had ended, she indicated that she had completed her Ph.D. and felt happy and secure. She indicated that she was no longer plagued by her husband's shadow, and had recently taken a position as a member of the board of directors of a regional organization.

In negotiating the Oedipal phase of development, the female has to concern herself with an issue which is the source of a specific type of guilt inherent in developmental movement: the shift of her love during this phase from the mother, the primary love figure, to the father. Why does the girl shift allegiance during the Oedipal period? The traditional psychoanalytic view is that the little girl, in seeking satisfaction from the mother, is frustrated and disappointed and turns to the idealized father. The belief that the father can alleviate the shortcomings of the mother provides the impetus for a change of affection by the girl. Psychoanalytic theory further postulates that unconscious psychological mechanisms develop and persist as attempts to solve problems. The little girl, to extend her own self-definition, must disengage herself from Mother by using Father as a vehicle. The father belongs to the mother, who is seen as hostile to the girl's interest in him. The girl renounces her desires and abandons the successful pursuit (and outcome) of these desires, since a successful outcome would engender intense guilt. Furthermore, the girl fears that the mother will abandon her unless she first abandons the possibility of victory. This failure to achieve what one desires is linked to the object of one's desire: a man. The girl, then, must abandon this aggressive wish for winning her father and return to the position of safety: that of identification with her mother and the sublimation of her desires.

This scenario continues: the girl turns to her father partly from an identification with her mother. The mother is admired, loved, and envied, but in the girl's mind this act of turning to the father converts her mother into a rival and potential aggressor. There is an elaborate constellation of directiveness and demands, rewards, and punishments, and a resultant identification not only with the superego of both parents but with the ideals and values of the idealized parents (2).

Psychoanalytic theory most commonly attributes the striving for motherhood as a representation of a female reproductive drive or as a form of compensation to achieve "wholeness." Another point of view maintains that the desire for motherhood may be a core feminine wish rooted in identification with the mother and corresponding with the incorporated maternal ego ideal of the girl (2). When there is a largely positive ideal, there is a greater likelihood of having a basic desire for children, and when the maternal ideal and earlier experience are largely negative, there is often little desire to have a baby. There are also deeply rooted maternal aspirations and ideals which evolve into other types of caring responsibility and humanitarian concerns rather than into the desire to have children. If this aspect of maternal identification is enmeshed in the competitive strivings of the girl, she may then be afraid to compete and achieve if it would directly conflict with her own ideal of femininity and womanhood.

The Oedipal conflict itself is universal. The resolution of this conflict may, however, be pathological. The child, girl or boy, at age four and five generally accepts the idea that the baby "comes from the mother's belly" but does not possess the kind of cognitive sophistication to understand the cause-and-effect relationship and implications of how it got there and how it develops. Direct observation of children of this age also indicates that the fantasy of carrying a baby is shared by both boys and girls, although it is much more strongly held by girls because of their identification with the mother. According to the observational studies, an identification with the mother by a girl of this age, rather than desire for impregnation by the father, seems the more plausible explanation for the fantasies of having a baby. Likewise, where compromised or conflicted relationships exist between a mother and a daughter of this age, there is disidentification rather than a tendency to identify with the mother and desire a baby, and the replacement of play with dolls by play which tends to emulate the father.

A woman who can never allow herself to match or exceed her mother's previous or current level of achievement may be perpetuating an Oedipal battle which she continuously loses. She feels that she must lose because winning would mean entering an incestuous battle with the mother for the father. She may, like Margaret, be able to achieve only in areas which her mother did not, or get *almost* to a position of parity with her mother and stop.

For many women as well as men, successful intellectual activity may be the unconscious equivalent of being "masculine," or succeeding in the Oedipal drama of attaining a status equal to (or better than) that of the father. A mother may assume the father's symbolic role for a girl in such a scenario. Guilt is engendered by this competitiveness and by having fantasies of surpassing the mother or even rivaling or dispossessing the father in his position of power.

One complication of the usual Oedipal situation occurs when deep and early maternal dependency needs are unmet in the first three to four years of life. As a result of maternal deprivation, the girl turns to the father for support to move ahead. This need for maternal love and comfort from the father becomes fused with Oedipal success. Closeness and success then become infused with guilt and may be taken away because the initial success occurred at the expense of the mother.

If a girl enters the Oedipal phase with a cohesive sense of self, alive and vibrant, the experience and expression of her Oedipal feelings still require appropriate parental responses for this developmental phase to be integrated and for development to proceed optimally.

A confluence of functional changes in the child biologically, perceptually, and cognitively during the sixth to eighth years of life permits the initial resolution of the Oedipus complex, the dominance of inner controls, and the evolution to a higher level of organization. There are greater stability and consistency internally at this point in life, as well as new cognitive structures which support better control of drives and postponement of action (3).

CHAPTER 7

Adolescence: The Emerging Self

CERTAIN DEVELOPMENTAL aspects occurring in adolescence have particular bearing on future achievement. Many biological, social, and psychological changes occur during adolescence: A resurgence of sexuality, aggression, independence, intense peer group pressure, and rapid biological change and physical maturity are among the many significant stresses upon the adolescent. The resolution of issues concerning body image, sexuality, and aggression directly affects the female's view of herself as a woman. Exaggerated or pathological defenses may develop; the involvement of others in an effort to create a solution to earlier difficulties may become more pronounced.

During this period, many factors can affect the girl's ability to integrate her feminine and sexual development with the rest of her personality development. Such major issues as the quality of the parents' marriage, the father's attitude toward women, the mother's attitude toward self-expression and autonomy, and the roles and opportunities provided by the society in general are all components in her own resolution of these developmental tasks.

74

During adolescence the form and image of her body evolve and mature into a consistent representation of femininity and womanhood. Puberty and the onset of menarche are important developmental landmarks. Ideally, the mother will help the girl during this period of vulnerability. Different attitudes will contribute to or inhibit the psychosexual development of the adolescent female. For example, menarche may be interpreted to be dirty, disgusting, and shameful. On the contrary, the girl may convert shyness and uncertainty into self-assurance and pride in her femininity, becoming expressive, assertive, and more expansive during this period.

The de-idealization of the parental image is one of the developmental tasks of adolescence. (This can be one of the most difficult and disillusioning periods for the parent to experience.) If the girl has career aspirations and the mother did not have such aspirations herself as an adolescent, it may be an especially difficult time for both mother and daughter, since the idea of a career will be a new element. As her own children move into adolescence, the mother may feel devalued personally if she has no career. The mother's struggle with this value system will have an impact on her daughter. It is difficult for the mother and, ultimately, the girl if the mother questions her own ideals and values. If the daughter is ambitious about a career, she may suffer unconscious guilt associated with turning away from the mother, her original love object, and the fantasies associated with this shift in loyalty.

The importance of the father's role for the developing girl has received insufficient attention. The father, for her healthy development, must be comfortable with a girl's femininity as well as with her potential to become a powerful person. The marital relationship as well as the ordinal position of the daughter in the family may significantly affect the father-daughter relationship. The father is the first man who is loved by the girl and the first man whom the girl competes with and for.

The admiring sparkle in the eye of the opposite-sexed parent has a great deal to do with what it is like to be boy or girl, man or woman. If the girl is a failure in kindling the proud, pleasurable, and envious interest of her father, the twinkle that says she is feminine and sexual, the deposit which she carries from this failure is the assumption that she may fail with other men. If the father's responses are inappropriate because of his own discomfort with sexuality and women, she may later find herself choosing inappropriate men, unable to be related to in a fulfilling way. One young woman described her precociously voluptuous physical development and the way her father responded to it. He had continued to treat her as a tomboy, and was more comfortable seeing her as a boy. (He had once bought her boy's pajamas when she was six years old.) When she was about thirteen years old, he took her hunting, a regular outing for them. After she successfully made a particularly difficult shot at a quail, he said, "Atta boy!" She turned to face him fully and stated, "Dad, I'm not a boy." She added (to me), "That was the last time he ever took me hunting."

A girl's preoccupation with matters of procreation, as well as a renewed interest in her father's regard for her, resurfaces with more intensity in early adolescence as an attempt to secure her female identity. Her femininity is confirmed by her father's acceptance of, and comfort with, her developing sexuality. His appropriate response allows sublimation of her unconscious fantasies of attraction to him.

Adolescent development has been characterized by Adelson and Douvan (1) as an experience of autonomy, assertiveness, and independence for boys and of the development of interpersonal competence for girls. If this is true, the core of identity for girls is formed by the development of interpersonal ties which may be impeded by active, direct expression of assertiveness or even feminine sexuality at times. The intimate friendships formed between and among girls paradoxically help them to find their individuality. It is from interpersonal relationships that individuality and identity are consolidated and an individuated personal identity is formed for girls during adolescence. For boys, identity solidification in adolescence involves disconnecting and separating themselves from parents in order to be distinct. The boy's sexuality is less dependent on a fully developed relationship (2). For mature individuation and sexuality, the consolidation of a satisfactory identification of the boy with his father, and the girl with her own mother, must be clarified and assumed.

When there is unmanageable parental or societal resistance to achievement of increasing independence and internal autonomy, the adolescent girl may become rebellious. If there is internal conflict around such issues as dependency, an adolescent's rebellion may persist into adulthood. For example, a provocative manner which creates irritation and annoyance may characterize work behavior. Discharge or demotion may be the outcome of this rebellious position, giving the impression that the individual seems incapable of keeping a job for prolonged periods of time. In a longitudinal history, a struggle with authority figures may become a recurrent theme, and the perception of the demand imposed by authority figures becomes the opposite of pleasure. Work for a rebellious individual of this type resembles duty; it is a symbolic struggle involving dominance versus submission, obedience versus control (3).

There are generally two types of families which can create the rebellious adolescent. One has overly controlling and authoritarian parents who rigidly require adherence to rules which are perceived by the adolescent as arbitrary, capricious, and unfair. The young person then experiences conflicts over his or her own aggression, and feels intimidation and helplessness which are ameliorated only by rebellious power struggles. As an adult, the individual will transfer his or her perceptions of authority figures to other people, imbuing them with the same powers and attitudes as parents, and an unconsciously motivated rebellious scenario which recapitulates the childhood struggle will be established.

A second family type is quite the opposite: very little parental control, with inconsistent, weak boundaries and constraints, with little consistent external structure for the child to internalize as boundaries and self-controls. For this child, an absence of parental response or parentally established boundaries creates desperate attempts to provoke establishment of rules and boundaries. Responses are provoked by rebellious or destructive acts directed to the attention of parents or other authority figures. The resulting adult response is often harsh and critical, perpetuating the ambivalent fear of and wish for a guiding authority. One extreme instance of this position is the criminal who would rather be wanted by the police than by no one at all. Another example is the borderline mother who produces a borderline child (see discussion on page 37). The child may go to any extreme, including destructiveness, to evoke a parental response. Even if the response is negative, it may be more predictable and certain than loving responses. Psychological conflicts with authority are often entwined with a fear of success. Demanding, authoritarian, or perfectionistic parents may inflict humiliation or punishment upon a child who exhibits assertiveness and aggressiveness.

The choices of work and career, with their concomitant issues of autonomy and competence, are more potentially difficult for the girl to the degree that her family has been inflexibly "traditional." Past identifications, expectations, and conflicts regarding roles may resurface at this time. There may also be conflicting messages from those around the emerging young woman who wish her to do well, but not too well. Her family, as well as society, may demonstrate contradictory values and expectations, which may enhance her own ambivalence. In fact, the societal situation of the early 1980s has created a kind of double jeopardy for the developing girl. While it is still somewhat startling for her to say "I want to be a judge," it is no longer so laudatory for her to say "I want to be a mommy and have babies."

The developmental process is lifelong. While the early mother-child relationship has immense impact, and the father-child relationship has a significant impact, these only lay the foundation for relationships with people of both sexes. The blocks built upon that foundation are the continued developmental process. If the foundation is weak or unbalanced it will affect the building process and ultimately the building. The manner in which the individual solves early developmental problems concerned with a sense of self, relationships with others, psychosexual development, and intrapsychic maturation determines the thrust and direction of further growth and personality development. Successful management of later biological crises, such as puberty, menopause, pregnancy, serious illness, and aging, as well as environmental demands, such as emancipation from one's family, following a career, motherhood, and widowhood, depends upon an integrated self and sufficient ego strength to master new situations in a creative and vital way.

SECTION III

Success and Success
Inhibition

CHAPTER 8

———◆———

The Development of Work Identity and Self-Esteem

THE CHILD'S CONCEPT of work and career can be expressed in fantasies regarding adult activities and in a desire to grow up. Actual interests, abilities, and pursuits are fashioned from these fantasies as the adolescent becomes a young adult. The complex vicissitudes of the interaction between the personality and the environment begin to focus in a career identity as early adulthood is approached. Many factors enter into the development of career identity: environmental opportunities, individual skills, special interests, and other particular features of the job market and educational experience.

Crucial internal components in this important transition are the person's individual initiative, curiosity, aggressiveness, and sense of self. As an individual begins to crystallize these aspects of her self-concept into work and a career, it becomes readily apparent whether these factors facilitate or impede her growth.

An identity is formed in work and career which becomes an important pillar in the structure of self-esteem. This transition to a "work identity" and a career occurs within a matrix of total personality development. The healthy adolescent urges herself toward mastery and accomplishment. Erikson (1) calls this phase—when the individual enjoys recognition and increasing self-esteem for productivity and self-sufficiency—the "sense of industry." If this work identity does not create a positive sense of self-esteem, compromises which offer less gratification and status become a source of depression or mental disturbance.

The emergence from a supportive family and structured academic surroundings into a more impersonal and less structured work world may produce confusion and hence anxiety about one's self-image. The young adult woman from the traditional family may have difficulty when her ego ideal is not in consonance with the assertive, competitive things she must do in work. The woman with perfectionistic expectations and a harsh superego demanding superhuman achievement may rapidly feel discontent, severe self-doubt, and failure. The woman who wishes to have a child and be a dedicated mother experiences discomfort and dissonance if she has an equally strong desire to dedicate herself to the vigorous pursuit of career advancement.

Many facets of personality development impinge upon career achievement and the crystallization of a work identity. Work identity and its associated personality structure are so important in the psychic life of the individual that they may cause upheavals in non-work areas not necessarily having great impact on work functions. (2)

Males and females characteristically have had different developmental lines and transitions from adolescent and academic activities into adulthood and career. The uniqueness of the emerging self and the realm of work and achievement for the woman have been emphasized insufficiently. The healthy woman's adult work expectations and achievement become integrated into her personality and are consolidated as an area of autonomous functioning. The core of the self and its associated self-confidence, self-esteem, initiative, and motivation are established during childhood and through adolescence, solidifying at this transitional time into a woman's belief in her effective, affective, and instrumental position in her own life and in the world.

The external forces that oppose the realization of career dreams for women have diminished, allowing a clearer view of internal forces which sometimes actively impede achievement.

These forces will be examined as they impinge on women and as this bridge to adulthood is built and crossed.

The Bridge to Adulthood and Achievement

A climate of free self-expression encourages the growing girl to explore numerous types of interpersonal relationships, behavior styles, and activities without gender-related constraints. This climate is provided initially by parents and is represented by the *process* of interaction of the parents with each other and with the child. The *content* of interaction is less important, since the child perceives and internalizes what is *done* much more profoundly than what is *said*. The parents' expectations for a girl will, hopefully, not be narrow, and they will be able to praise her success in a wide range of areas, rather than constricting her horizons by responding positively to only a very limited number of arenas of achievement. Many other factors will impinge on this process, including the ordinal number of the girl in the family. For example, the first child is usually a greater object of parental hopes, anxieties, and pressures to achieve than later children (3). The parents are more eager for the first child to validate their own self-worth. Firstborns are more likely to receive more education, and more likely to achieve greater success and eminence.

There are multiple, complex determinants which interact in developmental movement toward achievement and successful work. The following studies are especially useful in illustrating some of the common themes in the families of girls who grew to be accomplished, successful, and emotionally healthy as adults.

The family dynamics of extremely successful female executives were studies by Hennig (4). Common factors were sought which may have facilitated their success early in life. The women in the sample reported perceptions of their parents as warm and attentive. In particular, they viewed their relationships with their mothers as warm and supportive, and more or less "typical." The perception of the father was clear and consistent: there was a much warmer, more supportive, and more sharing relationship than between most fathers and daughters. This sharing included the father's interest as well as actual participation in the child's activities and endeavors. These women also saw a particularly strong relationship between the parents as well as between child and parent. Perception of this strong relationship between the parents included the feeling that they had a great deal of mutual respect for each other as persons and as contributors to the family.

These findings indicate an absence of standard sexual stereotypes within the subjects' families and a lack of the girl's traditional sharing of common interests predominantly or solely with the mother. The study's results challenge the general belief that an achievement-oriented woman is simply "raised like a boy."

The most important finding is the evidence of consistent support from both parents for the girl's freedom of exploration and expression. The fathers regularly participated with the daughters in all activities and extolled the ability to choose one's activity regardless of role designation; both parents supported and engaged in aggressive and competitive activity with their daughters. There was no sacrifice of the individual characteristics of either sex. The joint activities were perceived as defining a *person* rather than as defined by the boundaries of being a *girl*. Parents encouraged the girl to establish her own goals and standards for measuring herself and her achievements, rather than having boundaries set by a gender stereotype. The result of these experiences was personally determined reward and satisfaction.

Another interesting family dynamic identified in this study was the resolution mechanism in gender-related role-definition conflicts. When the subjects of this study began school, they encountered constraint and at times punishment for engaging in active and aggressive behaviors and were restricted to more passive activities. The parents responded by requesting school authorities to lift these restraints. Once again, the process which the child observed was extremely important, in that it represented support by the parents of her values and abilities, which in turn encouraged her expression and expansion.

A common denominator in the families studied was the fact that both parents valued the daughter for both femaleness and successful achievement. Moreover, both parents valued each other as people, played equally important roles in the family, and supported the roles and abilities of the other. Each parent related to the child as a separate individual, not as an extension of himself or herself, which would infer imposing one's own wishes, ideas, and feelings on the child. It was continually emphasized, not only in word but in the process of interaction, that the options available to both sexes were available to the girl.

Lozoff (5) also found that successful women had positive identifications with both mother and father. These women envisioned their future as one in which they would grow personally and in a relationship. In contrast, the group with least autonomy and vocational success defined success in the context of vicarious identification with the success of husband and children. The group of "autonomous developers" in this study had dynamic and ambitious fathers *and* mothers. Most of the autonomous developers described themselves as emotionally similar to their fathers and able to disagree with the father and his values. Foremost among the qualities which these women felt they shared with their fathers were assertiveness, outspokenness, and an ability to understand behavior rationally and make intelligent plans. *The fathers of the autonomous developers treated both sons and daughters alike in respect to their ability and value and encouraged freedom of expression in development according to individual interests and inclinations.* It is important to note that in this study population, fathers encouraged daughters to develop autonomously, without linking sex roles to their behavior or constraining them within gender stereotypes. The fathers still conveyed to these girls a strong sense of value as females, and as women. The women in this group demonstrated the most comfort with their femininity and sexual identity.

There is also evidence that the women in this study perceived their mothers as somewhat ineffectual and inadequate. Lozoff's evidence indicated that this perception changed with the attainment of the girl's own ambitions. As freshmen in college, women described as autonomous and independent characterized their mothers as somewhat colorless, inadequate, and uninformed. After graduation these same women described their mothers as having such characteristics as "strength of opinion" and "wisdom." One conclusion that could be reached is that Oedipal coloring competitively reduced the effectiveness perceived in the mother initially. Later, when Oedipal issues were probably mitigated by the girl's own maturation, independence, and equal status, she would have no further need to competitively diminish her perception of her mother and would be able to see her more accurately.

These studies illustrate the significant force and development of the ego ideal. The ego ideal is the image of the self to which an individual orients and aspires, both consciously and unconsciously. It is the ego ideal against which the woman measures herself. The ego ideal is based on identification with both parents and other early significant others. To the extent that a person does not measure up to her own ideal, self-esteem suffers. Shame is the usual affect accompanying the failure to fulfill one's ego ideal (a transgression of the superego, the internal voice mitigating ethical standards, creates the affect of anxiety based on guilt).

The development of self-confidence comes from approval for the child's independent initiative, from consistent support, and from nurturing of autonomy. Assistance from the parents to support the child's development of internal confidence is an early part of its foundation.

Character structure undergoes a major solidification in the transition from adolescence to adulthood. Personality characteristics and patterns, as well as potential psychopathologies, emerge in some clinically consistent ways. Some illustrative types of struggles in women who are destined for problems in achievement will be discussed below.

The Imposter Phenomenon

CASE STUDY

Laura, age thirty-five, came to treatment after two significant events: the recent death of her mother and a major promotion at work that involved considerable managerial responsibility.

Although she had realized one of her major aspirations with this promotion, she became acutely anxious and began doubting her ability to perform. She described the two "selves" she experienced. One ("my real self") was seen as good—an approximation of her ideal. The "other woman" she experienced as a kind of imaginary companion who emerged whenever her disallowed erotic or aggressive urges warranted expression. The crystallization of her discomfort occurred when she could no longer compartmentalize her two selves. The anger and sadness caused by her mother's death and the recognition of her assertive position in her own career made it no longer possible to unconsciously delegate her unacceptable impulses and affects to "the other woman."

She began feeling as if she were a facade, a fake, or as she put it, as if "I am not really me." She began to question whether she could be competent in her new capacity. Her doubt grew about her promotion being a token promotion, for her company had no women executives at her level. Her doubt and anxiety affected her concentration at work, and she began to retreat more and more to her private office. She increasingly avoided delving into major commitments at work. She used the observation of her doubt, anxiety, and retreat as validation that her conclusion of being inadequate for her job was a correct assumption.

Her advancement at her job coming at the same time as her mother's death brought forth her unconscious Oedipal competition. There had been much unspoken competition between Laura and her socially prominent mother during Laura's childhood and even in her adulthood. The mother, apparently valuing physical attractiveness a great deal, saw both the ageing process and her attractive daughter as a threat to her self-esteem. At the beginning of Laura's adolescence, the mother had an affair, and she withdrew from active support of Laura at this time. The mother's comment when Laura had announced two previous promotions had been to warn her about the economy and the precarious position of her company rather than to actively applaud her achievement. Laura's current anxiety and depression were the manifestation of this conflict, which she had attempted to repair since early childhood by disassociating into a "not-me" and "me." She disavowed her achievement as "fake" as a protective nonrecognition of her accomplishment. Unfortunately, the promotion and the mother's death were both resonant with this unresolved issue for Laura. The concurrence of these two events proved overwhelming for her.

Laura used treatment to look at the origins of her feelings of inadequacy and of being an imposter. "I fantasize that a man thinks I am wonderful. There are lots of superlatives: beautiful, capable, sexy. Someone who would make me feel good about me by his comments. I can't really have a fantasy without me in it. I have fantasies but they are not sexual fantasies. If I have a sexual fantasy, it is of 'the other woman' being sexy, seductive, and initiating things." She describes this "other woman" as a sort of imaginary companion who emerges at certain times. Laura described putting on a "company mask" for business affairs, with different facades for different circumstances. She accepted herself by perceiving each of the parts of herself when enacted and given the formal status of a role as not herself, "not me."

During the week, she attempted to hide her opulent possessions and her "other life" from co-workers and friends, feeling that she could fit into her work life and home life by keeping them completely separate. She and her husband had a weekend home at a resort, where Laura could feel free to be the "other woman." She wore designer clothes, expensive jewelry, and furs—none of which she kept or wore at her regular home. She could also be free in another way: she allowed herself to dress seductively and be aggressive sexually. Her husband was quite puzzled by her startling change in behavior on weekends and vacations. (Needless to say, they both found themselves wanting to spend more time at their resort home.) Laura experienced the weekends as the only time she could allow "the other woman" in her to emerge. Even at these times, she had to fantasize herself as actually being a different person—another woman who looked and acted differently from her. Her imaginary companion, whose bodily characteristics she could slip into, was particularly useful in her sexual relationship with her husband.

In order to internally manage these discrepancies, she needed to split off that part of herself which failed to measure up to the ideal so deeply etched in her from childhood. This split-off component, given the characterization of the "other woman," was the externalized participant evoked to express the unaccepted urges and feelings. She accepted only those aspects of herself which were attempts to remain without a flaw. She strove for perfection and imagined that "flaws" would be exposed with any awareness of what were, to her, unacceptable feelings, fantasies, or thoughts. To be less than perfect was to be considered flawed. Laura obsessively regarded any errors, perceived imperfections, or expressions of unacceptable affect as evidence of her being a failure. She rejected spontaneity and originality to become as predictable as possible. Creativity was decried because it was not standard.

Laura discovered in therapy the long-repressed origins of her duality. Her parents had been moralistic and perfectionistic, and were seen by Laura as having withheld praise and response. Even though Laura labored diligently to please her mother, the mother would focus on one aspect of Laura's efforts which needed improvement, rather than respond positively to her achievements. Her father was apparently somewhat crude although highly educated. He had difficulty relating to Laura in a warm, empathic manner. As she continued her strivings to achieve and please, they were never quite enough to win the hoped-for responses from her parents. Laura then developed an exalted, unobtainable ideal of perfection while concomitantly repressing her anger at her parents.

As Laura explored her duality in therapy, she discovered the adaptive purpose it had served earlier in her life and its current, daily maladaptive use. As treatment unfolded, she was able to resolve her conflicts and integrate both of her "selves" into a happy and productive whole.

———

PSYCHODYNAMIC ISSUES

The Imposter Phenomenon designates an experience of dishonesty in which high-achieving women feel that have "fooled everybody" (6). They see themselves as imposters and think they are not really very bright, despite outstanding academic and professional accomplishments. Their perception of themselves is not at all altered by objective evidence of superior accomplishment.

One study of patients in psychoanalysis offers a view of the changing manifestations of this phenomenon. Moulton describes comparison figures for two decades of adult female analytic patients (7). In the first decade of his study (the 1960s), of thirty-five cases of women in analysis, two-thirds had symptoms of sexual inhibition. In the second decade (the 1970s), when Moulton's paper was written, of a group of twenty-five very successful women in analysis, only five had symptoms of sexual inhibition but twenty-two had engaged in extramarital affairs. Thus the double life that some women lead has changed in its manifestation. The double life in the 1960s and earlier meant being a good mother and a diligent wife, but being severely inhibited sexually and in assertive expression. It appears that in the 1970s the double life had changed only externally; women had extramarital affairs instead of being sexually inhibited. Common to all of these women was an unusual amount of energy, competence, and capacity of self-assertion which remained unexpressed and/or disguised. Burying their potentials only deepened their resentment against the men in their lives. They held the men responsible for the inhibition of their assertiveness. The group of women who had extramarital affairs may have been expressing their desire for freedom as well as splitting off and disguising their resentment toward men (husbands) to whom they felt responsible and on whom they felt dependent. Both groups of women were dealing with a similar conflictual issue and fashioning double lives, even though the external manifestation was different.

The term "double life" which Moulton uses to describe a certain phenomenon has broad application. This duality exists whenever a woman orients her expression, direction, and values according to standards determined externally—by, for example, her mother, society, or her group of friends. When these standards of acceptability do not fit with what she is experiencing and do not allow unrestrained pursuit of her potential, a dichotomy exists which has to be dealt with. Frequently some aspects of thought, feeling, and fantasy are repressed or suppressed in an attempt at adaptation.

In the above study, Moulton describes the layers of unconscious factors found most frequently in a group of women with double lives. She explains the psychodynamic background for the overt behavior of the double life as consisting of:

1. A particularly ambivalent relationship with the father, who would initially encourage professional ambitions in a girl, only to later withdraw his support.
2. A negative identification with the mother, who did not supply satisfactory closeness in a girl's pre-Oedipal development, and who was threatened by and jealous of the girl's relationship with her father.
3. Deeply rooted dependency needs.

These dependency needs form the most primitive layer of character structure. They result from the lack of a supportive environment, maternal nurturance, and a positive role model for a feminine identification. While all three components described by Moulton occur simultaneously, pathology may be focused more in one area than in another. Maternal deprivation, for instance, may lead to a negative and conflicted relationship with the mother, accompanied by the need for a stronger and more positive relationship with the father. In turn, a positive, supportive, and "maternal" relationship with the father may result in more profound alienation from the mother, thus exaggerating the Oedipal rivalry.

Hidden Dependency

CASE STUDY

Sue, age twenty-seven, and her husband of four years, Bernard, thirty, had been discussing the possibility of having a child for several months. Bernard was quite vocal about being ready, while Sue was surprisingly reluctant. She began to ruminate about having a baby; thoughts about being pregnant and a mother obsessively intruded more and more into her waking time.

Her work in special education began to suffer as she became preoccupied and anxious with thoughts of having a baby and being a mother. She became worried that she was not a good teacher and that she would not be a good mother. The possibility of being a mother seemed terrifying and awesome to her. Her anxiety became more circumscribed over the next several months. Concerned about gaining weight, she concentrated on her caloric intake and rigorously limited her food consumption. Within a year she had gone from 122 to 92 pounds. Along with her weight loss, she became amenorrheic, thereby unable to have a child.

She presented for consultation after an appointment was initiated and planned by her mother. She appeared to be in an emaciated and almost childlike state. She looked extremely thin and delicate. She had emotionally and physically retreated to a time when she could suspend mature responsibilities. Her husband and her parents had increasingly taken over many of her functions and were now watching her closely and taking care of her; they were immensely concerned with what she ate. The ultimate threat by the family was that she would have to be fed if she did not feed herself.

She recognized during treatment the many ways in which she had attempted to avoid taking responsibility and demonstrating self-confidence. While she had been functioning in a seemingly competent way as teacher, wife, and homemaker, she had had an underlying fear of change, of responsibility, and of new endeavors. Her husband made decisions for her, sheltered her from assuming major responsibilities, and did things for her that she was capable of doing for herself. Thus he became the current version of her parents, who had taken a similar role earlier in her life. Indeed, she had transferred directly from her parental home to a home with her husband without being physically on her own.

Pregnancy and childbearing would not, in her mind, allow her further suspension of her protracted childhood and prepubertal status. She was consciously aware of her doubts about her ability as a mother. Emotional time was frozen for her, but her dependency had been veiled until she was confronted with motherhood. She regressively slid back to what she saw as a safer time, emotionally and physically. She became afraid of letting go, to eat what she wanted, as well as to be orgiastic sexually. At a deeper level, she unconsciously equated taking in food and having a full stomach with a primitive fantasy of getting pregnant orally and having a baby inside her.

In largely abstaining from food, she insured against what she saw as the ultimate step to being a full-fledged woman.

PSYCHODYNAMIC ISSUES

The hidden dependency in some women, even particularly ambitious women, may lead them to demand reassurance from men, and when it is not forthcoming, to feel deprived and uncertain, as if the men were the amalgamation of depriving parents. A women may seek support from different men, including a husband, a colleague, or others. The reinforcement she receives balances her self-doubt, but the perception of a need to be dependent makes her feel ambivalent and at times hostile about getting such reinforcement. With this conflict, the woman finds herself feeling the need for support and gratification of her dependence, but angry and resentful of it at the same time, ensuring her dissatisfaction.

In regard to dependency, it is not unusual to see mother and daughter show the same coping style and value system. For example, both mother and daughter may believe that women are incompetent and unvalued without a man. The mother may expend conscious effort in encouraging her daughter's use of creative energy to acquire a man rather than to fulfill herself in other ways.

The woman with hidden dependency needs may encounter severe problems in the assumption of responsibility, power, or authority. The woman with excessive dependency may be identifying with and reenacting a relationship with a pre-Oedipal mother. Since this model precludes equal cofunction, the overly dependent daughter who takes on responsibilities must unconsciously identify with the omnipotent mother. This experience is anxiety-provoking as she reexperiences the feelings of ineptitude and impotence which she suffered as a small girl in confronting her powerful mother. A reversal may ensue, in which, by means of sarcasm or criticism, she places others in a role similar to her earlier one, thus reenacting her trauma in a reversal of roles.*

The Traditional Woman in a Contemporary World

Among the characteristics of the "traditional woman" described by DeRosis (8) are some of the following: She depends on others for a primary sense of security, tries to please and avoid argument, needs external approval, maintains harmony and does not express anger easily, can be very skilled and competent but needs to discredit herself, is other-centered, expresses opinions apologetically, identifies others' needs as more important than her own, mostly is nonassertive, and will hesitate to accept leadership roles but can work behind the scenes.

Some women experience strong conflicts regarding traditional values and ideas. Their internal values and beliefs established in early life may undergo transition because of social

---

*This dynamic mechanism of identification with the aggressor and reversal of roles is common in mental functioning and accounts for many events we daily take for granted. Traumatic events are created in a repetitive way to attempt a belated mastery. Children who were beaten excessively will usually grow up to be child-abusing parents. A different outcome of this kind of reversal is represented by the parent who had an extremely difficult and impoverished childhood and attempts to give her own children everything so that they will not undergo her experiences—and, ultimately, so that her own experiences will not be relived or confronted through her children.

changes. A girl of traditional rearing emerges as a woman into a contemporary world. More recent events confront these internal values and create a dual pressure for the contemporary woman. She is confronted with the unconscious set of values and ideals of an early time juxtaposed currently with conscious demands and new ideals. She can be disillusioned when she sees that freedom is not license and equality is not entitlement.

It is not difficult to see how changing roles can evoke guilt and conflict for some women. Successful earlier adaptation to encompass stereotyped traits leaves little room for independent thought and action for some women. The traditional view, at one extreme, demands a self-effacing deference to others; the other extreme requires assertiveness. The qualities inherent in the expression of traditional characteristics are not limiting, since their overt goal is loving and considerate concern for others. Limits and constrictions do emerge, however, from overly strict adherence to these beliefs. The traditional woman may experience dissonance with her own ideal if she attempts to resist or alter her orientation.

If a woman has formed her ego ideal and her self-concept using a traditionally passive-dependent female model, her esteem may be diminished when she recognizes and expresses aggression or assertiveness, or even sees herself as too successful or too competent. She then experiences a sense of failure—failure to live up to her own ego ideal, which she unconsciously equates with success. When she unconsciously perceives success to be quite different, she is despairingly confused.

Willingness to renounce one's own achievements while applauding the achievements of a significant other characterized the "ideal woman" prior to the last decade or so. Women had to repress anger and aggressive impulses aggravated by these extreme requirements. Many individuals felt obligated to abandon their own aspirations to maintain a sense of security and certainty about themselves, their husbands, and their families.

Taken by surprise when confronted with situations calling for assertive positions and protection of her rights, a woman may respond in an effective or inappropriate way, feeling puzzled and perhaps angry at the result. For example, she may break into tears when she needs to express herself firmly. Response to the need for aggression with the language of dependency, e.g., tears, is both ineffective and regressive (9). The need for (and language of) dependency is a coping mechanism which a woman may resurrect an an expression of supposed weakness and helplessness. A different modality for dealing with aggression is available from earliest childhood for males. Unfortunately, the origins of conflicts over dependency and the ingrained expression of these conflicts are unconscious, and in many cases cannot be simply unlearned or consciously relinquished like a bad habit. Direct, or at least thinly veiled, aggression has been an accepted way of life for the boy since earliest childhood.

Ineffectively responding to a situation that calls for self-assertion, a woman may feel righteous anger and indignation with an accompanying sense of unfair treatment. She may even feel that she is being discriminated against because she is a woman. The discrimination may or may not be objectively true, but it is nonetheless her perception since *the necessary step of effective mastery was rendered ineffective by internal inhibition.*

Ingrained dependency in the traditional manner and its assumption of ultimate caretaking by a significant other is complicated by an abiding fear of antagonizing the caretaker; should this occur, the fear is of losing his care, being alone and helpless. This kind of fear has been the glue holding marriages together for some women. Their righteous anger or impotent rage may be expressed through helpless tears, replicating the infant's power over the parent. This problem, if deeply rooted, does not become resolved by the woman's simply learning to speak up or become assertive. Assertiveness is a behavior; the behavior can be a counterphobic expression of conflict without resolving the conflict. Approval from others is no longer the motivating desire.

Another manifestation of this conflictual dependency has been pointed out by Symonds (9). A woman who functions quite competently in a professional or business environment may be intensely dependent in relationships with men outside the work arena. The demand to be taken care of may even eventually jeopardize her work situation if it does not remain encapsulated in her love life. With this kind of need, a woman may attach herself to a man who is unconsciously trying to repress this need in himself, and in so doing presents an image of hypertrophied independence and autonomy. Only later do the latent issues become manifest and sensed by both partners, often dissolving the relationship. The illusion of each meeting the other's needs is exposed, and dissatisfaction is generally apparent.

A traditional woman may obtain little satisfaction from her achievements as long as she does not attract a man. Much of this woman's life has been oriented toward men: being attractive and pleasing, and finding a husband. Her self-respect may be determined by the value reflected in the eyes of men. Paradoxically, the woman who orients herself to a man's approval may now be threatening to this same man because of her competence. This woman may have had a mother with low self-esteem, who transmitted the message that women are insignificant unless possessed and defined by a man. A woman who is threatening to certain men because of her competence and aggressiveness finds herself in the contradictory position of unconsciously needing to seek out just the type of man who will be threatened. When such a man is threatened by her competence, the woman will withdraw from her relationship with him, in fear of being destructive to him (and ultimately thereby to herself). Conflict may be avoided for the time being. However, as in other repetition compulsions, the ultimate conflict is not resolved, because the woman is only dealing with conscious derivatives of it. Thus the struggle perpetuates itself, with dim hopes for a better solution the next time around.

Why is a man picked by a woman for reinforcement of her sense of self? Why do other basic issues hitchhike on sexual ones? One of the answers lies in the young girl's turning from the mother, if she is inadequate to foster self-development in her daughter, to the father for support and care. This establishes the father as the hoped-for source of nurturance instead of the mother. A girl in such a situation may grow up to be a "nagging" wife whose demands upon her husband are angry and endless, since she is acting on the fantasy that the man has something powerful which he is not sharing with her.

A woman may get an alternate sense of power over men by having a succession of lovers. This sense of power may be compensatory for feeling powerless and unacknowledged as a person now and/or in early life.

Early positive experiences with the father establish him as a prototype: he is not only the first man who is loved by the girl, but also the first man who is competed with and for. Positively supported experiences in self-expression, and in competitive achievement with males, establish comfort with, and mastery in, such encounters for the future.

If the mother cannot acknowledge or feel pride in her daughter's broadening accomplishments, the daughter may find it impossible to achieve success, feeling unsupported or even abandoned. The daughter may allow herself to achieve only in areas not undertaken by the mother. For example, the girl may not be able to get married, representing the ultimate extension of the Oedipal phenomenon. A woman may not be able to do more than her mother, feeling unable to bear the burdens of both family and career. She may find it necessary to disidentify with her mother by engaging in activities foreign to her mother's experience.

There may be conflicting desires, such as a wish to have a baby and a wish to develop a career. The decision, if it is between the two, is conscious, and there is not an obvious outcome or foregone conclusion as in past times. The decision to have a child may be either the *outcome of a wish*, and the fruition of one's ideal, or it may be a *defense*. Pregnancy and motherhood may, for example, be used as a solution to work inhibition; therefore, a baby and family could represent a sense of failure. Alternately, for some women, successful nurturance of a baby and family would fulfill life's highest ambition.

Some women experience a sense of incompleteness when they are alone, feeling existentially adrift unless someone else validates their "being" and importance. Although this narcissistic fear of being alone and engaging in solitary tasks will hitchhike on such reality issues as the danger of women doing things alone, upon psychological exploration it is often seen to be a fear of personal incompetence and sense of incompleteness. Presupposing their incapacity and inability, certain women do not venture out alone; this venture may be something as complex as starting a business or career, or something as basic as driving or going on short trips alone. Obviously such an internal organization will preclude venturing out in another sphere: the sphere of originality and creativity, since creative people and original thoughts explore areas where there is no predetermined structure. Creativity requires a freer access to intrapsychic and unconscious events, and boldness to venture into uncharted territory.

CHAPTER 9

$-\!\blacklozenge\!-$

The Psychology of Work

Play as a Precursor to Work

THE RELATIONSHIP of play to later adult functioning is important, and serves as the basis for developing interpersonal skills, the ability to interact with others socially, and an internalized belief in mastery of tasks. The developmental line of work has its origins in the beginning efforts of an infant to master, through play, herself and her environment. Erikson (1) emphasizes competence as a virtue developed in childhood which "characterizes what eventually becomes workmanship."

Children play for the conscious pleasure of it—because it is fun. In part, the fun of play is the experience of mastery. The purpose of play for children has been referred to by Piaget as "functional pleasure" (2). White calls play the "feeling of doing something, of being active or effective, of having an influence on something" (3). Murphy observed different responses in children who, from birth, did things for themselves as opposed to having another do it (4). She observed that children's capacity to enjoy themselves and their activity was closely connected to a sense of triumph: "I can do it." The satisfying feeling of "bliss" in being the passive recipient of efforts by another is distinguished from the joy of triumph and mastery in oneself and in one's activities. This satisfaction is particularly associated with play and work. The experience of positive mastery and triumph is a gratifying exchange with one's environment, and leads to further eagerness and motivation to respond to the environment as well as the optimistic expectation of future mastery.

One aspect of play is based on the process of the mastery and management of anxiety through fantasy. Traumatic experiences of the past or present, anticipated traumas, and internal conflicts are reproduced in play. This attempt to master conflict or trauma in an active rather than passive way is the essence of a variety of coping styles. Sublimation and symbolization develop as ego functions in part by the use of play as a developmental process of dealing with instinctual and affiliative needs. Fantasy and play act as "safety valves" which spare more open conflict with people and the environment (5).

In an examination of childhood precursors to the adult capacity to work, Cotton (6) observes that the level of maturity is what distinguishes work from play. She notes that "work" as revealed in the preschool child's play consists of imitations of adult mannerisms and roles and identifications with certain adult characteristics including strength, power, and beauty. The distinction between work and play for the child is an adultomorphic conceptualization. The preschooler's differentiation between play and work apparently revolves around the perception of adult status and reality (6). The childhood arena of play and the characteristics of play form the foundation of what will later be adult work and play and determine whether the two can be comingled.

Play does many things. Play provides the opportunity for the child to develop mastery over a traumatic event by repeating the event until it becomes detoxified and mastered. A child, after returning from a visit to the doctor or the hospital, may play-act visiting the doctor numerous times until her anxiety is sufficiently assuaged. There may even be, beginning in latency when abstract thinking is established, an anticipatory mastery perfected through playing. Play is a natural mechanism for mastering the child's world as well as anxiety-provoking experiences in everyday life. Playing can also be used to repeat gratifying experiences for recapitulated enjoyment.

If the arena of playing is constricted, however, by internal conflict or sex-role stereotypes, restricted or directed because of parental pathology, later adult work might be compromised. Also compromised might be the analogues of childhood play: mastery of the environment, a sense of competence, and the ability to cope with and manage stress which solidifies ego strength.

The capacity to work involves more than simply symptom-free functioning for both adults and children. While intrapsychic conflicts may compromise the capacity to play and work, the absence of such conflicts is not a sufficient factor for pleasurable and effective work and play for the adult (6). Work can satisfy a variety of psychological needs. Among the more important psychological aspects is its function in the consolidation of self-image and identity. It is a source of gratification and expression of ambition and creativity. Work also expresses values and beliefs, fosters self-validation, serves defensive functions, and offers relief of guilt or escape from the other life stresses (7). Work can also be seen as a sublimation of aggressive impulses, as the product of the urge to mastery. Formulations about work must consider all types of work, from many points of view.

Work Inhibition in Children and Adolescents

Halpern (8) has demonstrated the correlation between psychodynamic and cultural determinants of work inhibition in children and adolescents and work inhibition in adults. Most often, the symptom of work inhibition in children and adolescents is manifested in poor academic performance. One childhood syndrome which is a precursor to work inhibition in adults is due to disrupted separation and individuation. The success of childhood work life is correlated with the degree of separateness and individuality in the evolving development of the child as distinct intrapsychically from her parents. The progression of exploration, the triumph of skill, the demand for privacy, and the selection of goals are components of this individuation and the child's sense of separateness from parents.

Halpern found two types of parental pathology which predispose children toward work inhibition. In one pattern, one or both parents are narcissistic, excessively controlling, and center activity around themselves and their needs. In these situations, the child must either comply or use extreme measures to attain distinctness. For example, a child may experience her parents as overinvolved with her in a controlling way, as if her separateness were threatening to them. She may then refuse to achieve through school or work in an attempt to define a boundary between herself and her parents. Her failure to achieve may be seen as the only way she can carve out her own area of autonomy. She seeks distinctness from her overly involved parents by *not doing* rather than by *doing*. She makes an irrefutable statement to them that she is *not* an extension of them or their desires. In extreme cases, a child may feel that almost every accomplishment is in the service of the parents. Inhibition of achievement is seen in this instance as an attempt at individuation. Since the type of directiveness in the parents is often subtle and difficult to focus upon, it is difficult for the child to target efforts at individuation in an effective manner.

The second pattern of work inhibition in children described by Halpern is due to a pathological resolution of an intensified Oedipal conflict, with its resulting fears. As is the result for the first pattern, extreme efforts toward individuation must be expressed in a negativistic, self-defeating, or passive manner.

Halpern's study illustrates that emotional separation is a prerequisite to developing the capacity to make independent decisions about oneself and one's future, as well as establishing intimate relationships with others. A gradual, stepwise, and phase-appropriate diminution of the parents' involvement with the child is concomitant with an increase in the child's autonomy. When parents react to the child's natural moves toward independence as though she were abandoning or competing with them, the child may feel insecure about her normal growth processes and experience separation anxiety.

One symptom of separation anxiety is school phobia. This anxiety may manifest as upset stomach or some other illness which abates only when the child and mother are reunited. The child's avoidance of school to ward off her anxiety at leaving

Mother is half the problem; the other half is the mother who disallows autonomy and exerts a subtle, often unconscious, regressive pull on the child in an effort to deal with her own anxiety.

It is clear that the child's self-esteem and self-concept are affected by the moods and attitudes of her parents. If the mother is depressed or not interactive with the child, or if the father is preoccupied with his work, or often away, the child seeks an explanation. The child often concludes that she must be unlovable. Clearly, children of divorced parents or victims of abuses suffer most from this syndrome. The child concludes that she must be a thoroughly bad person to have been abandoned, abused, or chronically criticized. For the child, objective logic does not prevail at these times. If, for example, a father repeatedly chooses to play with his son rather than with his daughter, she may conclude that she is not as valuable a person as her brother. Most evidence indicates that girls who have the most difficulty in achieving self-esteem have unresponsive fathers and mothers who fail to act as a suitable model for feminine identification.

The role of the father in encouraging success may include his support of his daughter's competence in physical activity, intellectual accomplishment, and a host of other ways. If he later becomes afraid of the strength of her adolescent passions and cuts off the companionship that nourished her, the daughter may perceive this as a preference for a more demure, passive kind of woman. She must then conclude that something is wrong about herself. At this point she may feel abandoned or spurned, or assume that she is unattractive as a woman. Just the opposite may be the case: She may actually be too attractive to the father and therefore too threatening, too bright, or too tempestuous. Many instances of the severance of the relationship between fathers and creative, energetic daughters have origins at the start of adolescence. Her peers may also find her too advanced, and she may incite the jealousy of her fellow students if she is advanced scholastically. These experiences may further validate fears about being unfeminine and create doubt about accomplishment. Or she may unconsciously sense the disappointment of the father who wanted a son, and may strive unconsciously to be a good son for her father. "The Faster Dancer" (see Chapter 11) *concluded* that her father must have wanted a son, since he never responded positively and enthusiastically to her achievements. He was very vocal about her getting training for a job as a secretary or nurse, even though she was quite able and ambitious.

What Is Successful Work?

The answer to the question "What is successful work?" is as individual as each person. Generally speaking, there are several kinds of success in life. One type of success is in the development of warm and intimate relationships with both men and women. Another kind of success involves the development of skill and/or professional expertise. Yet another kind of success is productivity in the home as mother or as father.

Low (9) evolved a profile of successful women on the basis of a study she conducted. The women were independent, confident individuals who balanced achievement and femininity. Low noted that they were not devoid of conflicts but handled them in a particular way. For example, if they perceived unnecessary constraints, they would find alternatives which allowed them to proceed. Their self-esteem thus remained intact and provided a solid foundation for development. This study underscores the fact that it is not the absence of conflict which is essential but the ability to use adaptive measures when constraints emerge.

The following is a highly successful woman's reflections on the early childhood influences which she thinks may have had some direct bearing on the establishment of her potential for success:

> Looking back to my early years and many positive influences generated by my mother and father, it is not a simple task to isolate the influences that have had the strongest impact in determining my success as a woman today. Although I was the only child of my parents, I was raised with four cousins. The most impressive factor was the ideology of my father, which was catalyzed by my mother and respected by those adults with whom we, as a family, were in close contact. His position was to encourage me to speak my mind. My mother's position as the catalyst in relation to this was to allow me to do so, but to set down the ground rules. In other words, "think before you speak." She believed that speaking one's mind was not merely a matter of what is said, but just as important was the way it is said. . . . Through their encouragement of free expres-

sion of self, they enabled me to develop respect for myself. By insistence on my mother's part to be reflective, she was helping me to create the internal order necessary to facilitate motivation and the ability to set realistic goals for myself. Through repetition and consistency in their approach, they aided my development of self-confidence [and thus the process toward realizing those goals to proceed for myself.] Another factor that should not be overlooked is that my parents, through no preconceived plan, shared responsibilities in child rearing. . . . Still another contributing factor was the fact that once a week we spent the day together doing something as a whole family. This was a time of sharing, airing gripes, and just ordinary "catching-up." During these early years my mother taught me how to sew; my father and I sewed buttons on his shirts or my dresses or blouses when needed. Mother, through example, taught me care of my person and good grooming; my father taught me how to braid my hair. My father and I cleaned the house to surprise Mother and then worked on the car. Mother showed me how to fix electrical appliances; my father and I prepared dinner. Mother taught me how to make cakes from scratch; my father and I painted rooms in our house. (10, pp. 121-122)

The above account exemplifies how this woman grew up without stereotypes of female or male sex roles. It underscores the importance of self-expression, setting one's own goals, and the development of flexible, appropriate boundaries which foster self-development, as well as the importance of communication with others in developing understanding.

How are some women able to achieve remarkable degrees of success in the face of obvious obstacles? What is their sustaining motivation? How does this motivation differ for women applying their talents in business or a profession from the motivation of a bright, articulate, and gifted woman in suburbia who is mastering or even creating a new recipe or responding creatively to her children? Is there some implied value judgment as to which of these life-styles is preferable?

In any situation where achievement and success are in question, for both men and women, there is an ambivalent underlying anxiety about both success and failure. There are many individual dynamics which make each person's attitudes distinct. Although anxiety about success in men may differ from that of women, success for both men and women may usher in an anxiety about loss of dependency, increased responsibility, questions of capability, and loss of gratification from previous levels of attainment or roles.

Many women have not been reared to have the same sense of entitlement as men regarding their own personal and career growth. The careers of many men are nurtured by female caretakers: first the mother, often sisters, later a girlfriend, then a wife, then a secretary. The traditional woman is accustomed to excel in being supportive of others, but may overlook the nurturing of her own inner growth and development.

While the social atmosphere regarding women and careers has changed a great deal, self-images and identities may take some women longer to develop. For example, some women successfully identified with the national women's liberation movement as an attempt to replace an identification with a weak or passive mother. On the other hand, the contemporary woman whose choices and actions are dictated by "women's lib" may just as profoundly constrict herself as a woman who is totally constrained by traditional role models.

According to some studies, the mother is an important figure with whom to identify in ambitions, careers, and values. It was found that both sons and daughters of women in high-status positions achieved similar positions with much greater frequency than the sons and daughters in families where only the men had high-status positions (11). A positive result of the women's movement for many women has been the ability to identify with, and model themselves after, women who are ambitious and assertive. For others, it has simply loosened the restraining superego bonds, to allow into awareness and acceptance that which was perceived previously as taboo. However, the conscious awareness of women's issues is not enough if internal conflict or the more basic sense of self is organized around the feeling that one is less significant, less powerful, or less important than others, or if one is deeply identified with the idea of being pleasing to others.

Ideals and Identification

If one's ideal and identity conflict with the need to be assertive and aggressive, self-image and potential become compromised. child receives only punishment, never reward. It is the punishing image of someone who sees loving, kind feelings and assertiveness as being mutually exclusive. Valuing feminity but not letting it become a constraint is an important aspect in the development of the mature and successful woman.

The *content* and the *process* of the superego are helpful to distinguish and keep in mind in understanding self-image and realization of ideals. The *content* of the superego has to do with such things as the subjects on which one takes moral positions, the flexibility or rigidity of moral structures, the moral acceptance of sexuality, and the difference in the degree of aggression allowed expression. Generally, women have felt more guilty and ashamed of competitive feelings than men. Such competitive feelings may be directed toward other women or especially toward men; this stimulates an inhibiting function by the superego. Men may experience fear about competition, especially in the Oedipal situation with the same-sexed parent, but it is part of their ideal to compete successfully. The man is not likely to say "I am too competitive." The man is more likely to say "I am having trouble *being* competitive." The woman's ideal may include such content and value as being pleasing and useful to others and taking others and their values into account. The woman, therefore, is more likely to be swayed by personal considerations in making judgments.

The *function* of the superego of women in general may be due to a difference in relative values. Freud's position on the weakness of women's superego stated that because women lacked castration anxiety their superego would not be as sharply defined as men's. Guilt, Freud's reasoning went, would then not be as prominent in women, who would be more likely to develop shame, since shame is an affect growing out of narcissism. Freud basically felt that women were more controlled by shame and men more by guilt. The validation for his theory that the female psyche emerged in a welter of shame was the observation that women were not as ashamed to be afraid as men were.

The superego develops in a setting of reasonable, rewarding object relationships and reasonable frustrations. An ineffective superego develops, not necessarily in the absence of superego figures like parents for the child to incorporate, but when the To be successful and competent will not fit into the idealized self-without the concomitant experience of reward for positive endeavors that provides a no-incentive situation. There is no internalization of rewarding function and no consolidation of ideals: the internal view of how we wish ourselves to be. The result is a spotty consolidation of the superego—primitive and unorganized in certain areas and harsh in other areas.

An example would be the child who has experienced repeated failure at getting desired attention and loving response from her parents. Even her best efforts at pleasing often result in no response, positive or negative. Rather than experience the terrible loneliness and emptiness of this situation, the child soon learns that there is one consistent way she can get response from her parents: to be very bad. In contrast to her positive, helpful attempts to please, which result in inconsistent recognition, she can consistently get response by doing something destructive. Her primary aim is not destructiveness or masochistic behavior, but these become a vehicle for confrontation and for validation of her self. Moreover, her behavior gives her a sense of power and mastery, as opposed to the previous feeling of helplessness.

If a girl has a positive emotional experience with her father, as an autonomous and confident woman she will be free to choose a man who allows and encourages the continuation of her self-development. Women who have doubt and conflict within themselves may find mates who do not see them as unique and valued individuals and who denigrate their femininity and autonomy. This depreciation (or simply lack of expectation of autonomy and fullest functioning) is largely unconscious in many individuals and would be vigorously denied if confronted. The forms it takes may be illustrated by the assumptions residing within a household. These assumptions may be the uncontested decision of the husband in making financial or even vacation plans; or it may be assumed that the woman, if she chooses to have an outside job, will simply add it onto her usual household work.

Parents may want their daughters to be independent and successful, yet unwittingly give them signals to the contrary, emphasizing from an early age the importance of marrying and of pleasing a husband. Expansiveness and potency may be presented as destructive forces if they manifest themselves. To respond rather than to initiate may be deemed more appropriate.

One young woman who came for treatment was soon to graduate with a business degree. She was in a great deal of anguish about her ambivalence in wanting to be independent and have a career, yet fearing to leave home and function autonomously. She had not finished a number of projects required to obtain her degree. She concluded that she might have to postpone graduating. While her parents apparently encouraged her and were proud of her accomplishments, they also indicated to her that "of course if you can't make it or find a job you can always stay here and we'll take care of you." This young woman did not have the benefit of a mother who had encouraged autonomy throughout her life-cycle.

Current expectations of women to take up new roles may meet resistance from the past generation, who have not really experienced role emancipation themselves. It has been suggested that the near-epidemic manifestation today of bulimia and anorexia nervosa is an indication of the extreme ambivalence felt by some women regarding their autonomy. A woman with conflicts about aggression and competitiveness may perceive competition with an impact that is much beyond its reality. Those in authority, as well as equals, will then arouse aggressive feelings of competition which may, if inhibited or directed internally in a really destructive way, create a paralysis of effectiveness in work. The legacy of the ghost from competition past in the early family environment may prevent a conflict-free and uninhibited pursuit of goals.

It is often difficult to distinguish between the internal and external influences impinging upon women who seek careers and experience confusion in their pursuit. One aspect of this problem is simply time constraints; working mothers may do two jobs. Guilt about this can prevent some women from working until their children are in school. Other women may invest themselves quite deeply in their function as a mother because they believe this to be the most noble of all endeavors. Others may defensively retreat into motherhood, using this unassailable bastion as a retreat from other careers. This conflict can be further complicated by other emotional issues which are in resonance, such as the mother's anxiety keeping her from being away from her own children.

Pioneering work by the analysts Clara Thompson and Karen Horney in the 1930s and the 1940s focused on the dependent, affection-seeking, self-effacing, caring-for-others character structure traditionally linked to females, and the dominant, expansive, power-, prestige-, and possession-seeking, denial-of-feelings character structure traditionally linked to males. Both of these types of character structures may be, on the one hand, an acceptance of traditional cultural roles, but they also are solutions whose compromise-formation may have been influenced by the backdrop of stereotype and identification. Gentleness, tact, easy expression of tender feelings, and awareness of the feelings of others have not been the standard template for boys and men.

The role of work for women at various phases of the life-cycle involves the integration of autonomy and femininity, the capacity to sublimate rather than repressively defend against aggression, and the consolidation of feminine identity. Assertiveness and independence must be integrated with connectiveness and concern for others.

A woman may experience a lack of freedom to develop competency and self-expression in roles other than domestic ones. On an inhibition of creativity and innovation is overlaid efficiency, reliability, and competence in other skills, usually of acceptable domestic or passive-consolatory character. Lozoff (12) found that a group of women she called the "least autonomous" chose fields of endeavor where precision and diligence were rewarded, such as the teaching of grammar (as opposed to creative writing), the care of handicapped or helpless children, elementary school teaching, and nursing. Most of the women in the "least autonomous" group came from families where there were definite and at times rigid sex-role differences between the parents, where the fathers primarily supported their wives, and the wives acted to guide daughters toward good marriages. The mothers of these women were supportive, and enjoyed growth vicariously through their husbands and children.

A predominant fear and concern of the "least autonomous" group was of potential dominance. They assiduously avoided situations in which they might compete with men, and these women regarded vitality as unfeminine. They also were setting about to choose a husband who would claim superiority to them and who would support dependent, unassertive, and flattering women. These kinds of marriages obviously will work and achieve their own kind of equilibrium. They will work only as long, though, as the husband's power and unquestioned dominance is maintained; if and when the wife shows strains of her latent autonomy, a disequilibrium results.

There is an imputed gender-linkage of personality traits which affects men, just as another cluster of traits affects women. The limitations on ambition in women have counterpart stereotypic constrictions on sensitivity, emotional expression, and empathy in men. In families where it is not unmasculine for a boy or man to develop and express warmth, tenderness, and emotion, femininity is not at stake with the development of ambition in a girl or woman.

The family background of a man is related to his attitudes toward women as well. To the degree that this gender-linkage of traits has been previously established, a man may have difficulty accepting, acknowledging, and supporting a woman's ambition. When threatened by a woman's assertiveness and quest for independence, he may react with defensiveness: withdrawal, criticism, aggressiveness, or depreciation of her desirability as a sexual partner.

Gender-linkage of personality traits by a family (or later, a therapist) disallows empathic understanding of each individual's personal goals. The ability to recognize each individual's point of view and the flexibility psychologically to perceive a wide range of viewpoints and ideals are important. Individual goals outside stereotypic domains can then be pursued more freely. Consider, for example, the woman whose idea of success is a military career and achievement of an officer's position, as opposed to the woman whose ambitions are to be a warm and engaging mother who successfully rears children.

Marriage and Success Phobia

There are many women who feel satisfied and content *within* the confines of the stereotypical feminine role. Some, however, pay a price through considerable denial and repression of real feelings.

They may then choose to maintain rather than sacrifice their marriage or close relationship. The fantasy of abandonment if full self-expression is realized may have been insured in reality by the choice of a mate. The dilemma experienced is that of a compromise: either losing personal freedom or a spouse. Most often, however, this dilemma is experienced as coming from external circumstances; the woman does not recognize the profound internal conflict which colors the perception of other events and sets the stage and writes the script for enactment externally.

CASE STUDY

One woman who presented for treatment exemplifies this dilemma. Rosalyn, age thirty-two, had been married for ten years when she came to discuss how unhappy and depressed she had become, but focused on what she could do to help her husband, Bradley, with his own pressures and depression. He had, in the last seven years, formed his own company and had accumulated a net financial worth in the tens of millions. He was, however, experiencing extreme pressure in his business, and had developed hypertension and a duodenal ulcer. Rosalyn's complaint was that he related to her in a manner similar to the way that he ran the business: strongly dictatorial with no questions allowed. She felt confined, constrained, and as if she needed to function as an extension of his desires and wishes in order to maintain the marriage.

Bradley refused to have a joint evaluation with his wife and had earlier refused her entreaties to seek help.

As she began psychotherapy, she was able to unveil rather quickly many of the aspects of herself which could not be expressed in the marriage. She had been blinded to other points of view, as her own original family had functioned in a manner similar to the roles currently assumed by herself and her husband.

Within a few weeks of beginning treatment, however, she stopped. She had initiated an awareness of feelings, creativity, and independent thought and action which were threatening to Bradley. He indicated that continuing in therapy would result in a divorce. Rosalyn contemplated giving up the security of her marriage, her lavish, exciting, jet-set life-style, and decided to give up therapy. Her decision was so precipitous that she even disallowed herself time to discuss it in therapy.

Her focus remained on the external reality of an "either–or" choice. For her, the external issues were also metaphors for internal needs and fears which came too dangerously close to the surface.

PSYCHODYNAMIC ISSUES

Symonds describes a group of women who develop phobias or other types of constrictions after marriage (13). Women who are apparently independent, capable, and self-sufficient develop excessively dependent and helpless postures after marriage. Some do this suddenly and rather dramatically, such as in a sudden manifestation of phobias, while others may develop constricting symptomatology over a period of years. These women may become fearful of traveling, may be afraid to be alone, perhaps cannot drive a car by themselves, or may become extremely uncertain in taking responsibility and making decisions, feeling as if they need to cling to their husband for constant support. In this type of neurotic inhibition, the woman is first defending herself against putting into action some type of prohibited wish or impulse, with the expectation of danger or retribution should this occur. The anxiety of so doing is avoided by means of an inhibition: She gives up that which confronts or represents her urge or wish. For example, anxiety over separation and leaving home—relinquishing dependency on parents—is assuaged by a fear and avoidance of driving.

The price some women are willing to pay to avoid expressing anger or hostility is extremely great. A manifestation of this fear is a woman's seeming "inability" to communicate clearly with her partner, which protects her against direct and clear assertive effort. This woman may become "confused" and retreat in a passive manner from a confrontation. Ordinary assertion is fused with forbidden aggressiveness. The woman may tolerate extreme behavior on the part of her husband with no apparent protest, while presenting the picture of extreme compliance, even helplessness. The need to avoid criticism of her husband concomitantly requires the repression of anger, often leading to other symptomatic manifestations, such as psychosomatic disorders or depression.

The women Symonds describes, who were seemingly autonomous prior to marriage but who developed phobias after apparently successful marriages, had similar backgrounds. All came from families in which self-control of feelings was paramount. As girls, they had to behave like miniature adults; to play and act like children was not accepted. Developing "maturity" at an early age gave the illusion of strength and self-sufficiency; the need to be taken care of was repressed. Avoiding criticism from parents was paramount. Marriage for these women represented the opportunity to finally be dependent (now on their husbands) without self-criticism. Marriage then became the "declaration of dependence." The marriage was inevitably disappointing, since the institution does not speak to this basic need on all occasions—which further perpetuated the anger that had to be repressed at all cost.

The first step of this process is when a young, apparently strong and capable woman gives up her work, education, or profession upon marriage, to settle for the role structure of a traditional marriage. To survive, it is necessary for her to suppress assertive impulses, especially with men, for fear that she may endanger her hoped-for sense of security. Part of the price paid is the loss of spontaneity and development of her own autonomy, which are replaced by a fear of antagonizing those on whom she is "dependent." This same dynamic was earlier articulated in a study of a college population in which it was found that many girls' reaction to a significant crisis was apathy and dependence, a reversion to a manifestly needy and insufficient posture (14).

What is the role of childbearing? On the one hand there are certainly expectations from various sources, perhaps the more pressing ones being from the ego ideal of the woman, modeled after that of her own mother, which included childbearing and mothering as a supreme task. Even for the woman who truly wants to become a mother, there are issues related to a temporary cessation of her own career. The answers to this question are fashioned both internally and externally (between wife and husband), but nevertheless involve a kind of hiatus in the woman's career which the husband usually does not face. And the pressures from society include the very pronounced idea that a woman is expected to want a child or "something is wrong." Of no small emotional significance for some women is the fact that they may feel their adequacy and worth is proven by having a child or children.

The woman of today has a more conscious and real option of whether or not to bear children. This issue presents a dilemma. Previously a woman's life was organized around her concept of duty. To be comfortable in this role as wife/mother forced her to repress any dislike or resentment of the nurturing role and made her deny other yearnings. With other choices available, her life is more complex. Internal conflicts about various aspects of intra-psychic life come into play: living up to her ego ideal, anxiety caused by the guilt of not living up to her own internal model, ambivalence about forging her own decisions, fears of adequacy as a mother, intense feeling about the abandonment of another career.

There are some women who choose to be mothers yet never make it a "career," i.e., do not become involved or invested in motherhood. Their nominal involvement in motherhood includes relegating its functions to a surrogate such as a live-in maid, caretaker, or nurse. This is one solution to the dual-role conflict. Why is this woman choosing motherhood? Is she simply paying lip service to a model, ideal, and set of expectations in which she no longer believes? That is, it may be programmed within her from long ago that in order to be a complete and mature woman, she must be a mother. Responding to this ancient dictate, she then gives birth to children, but becomes aware that she does not want to *function* daily as a mother.

Erikson (15) states: "The mere attempt to right a wrong by turning it upside down and claiming that there is no instinctual need for parenthood and that parenthood is *nothing but* social convention and coercion will not liberate anybody's choices. A choice is free when it can be made with a minimum of denial and guilt and with a maximum of insight and conviction."

Women, much more than men, have traditionally taken more of their identity from the man whom they marry and with whom they live. Their choice of a partner has determined their locale, social functioning, and socioeconomic status. There is, however, much more of a selective process and determination of destiny than is consciously realized. A woman, consciously and unconsciously, determines the person she will marry, knowing (or in some cases, needing to deny or be unaware of) her husband's goals, ambitions, life-style, tendencies, and personal characteristics. Her own view of herself finds reciprocity in the selected partner. If a woman assumes an identity which *includes* equality in its fullest sense, then the relationship and her life may be much enhanced. This selection process includes selecting someone who can and will tolerate her as an equal, as autonomous, and as having internal freedom. If this cannot be tolerated by the woman, she will choose a man who also cannot tolerate it, perhaps seeing him as a source of repression. For example, if a woman assumes a masochistic posture she will then look for someone with a sadistic bent to complement it. (A sadist is someone who is kind to a masochist.)

Midlife Issues

Women in midlife who return to a career or who seek a career have to blow off the dust from the long-shelved final tasks of adolescent development. The major tasks confronted and worked through by women in this midlife return to work are the final steps of separation–individuation toward autonomy. It may be, after time and effort have been spent in motherhood and wifely tasks, that the woman in midlife allows herself a redirection toward her own development and fulfillment. It is as if the requisite time has been put in to fulfill the archaic expectations of the ego ideal, so that the woman, having met these "requirements," can now proceed to renewed development. Such a woman is more likely than someone who actually resolved rather than simply "met" these archaic expectations to continue to be a prisoner of stereotype in some veiled manner as she proceeds in her career. She is more vulnerable to the demands for attention from her husband and even her older children. The husband may be quite involved in his own career and quite resistant to evolving changes in his wife and home. Her own deeply entrenched identifications with her mother may have to be partially grieved and given up, especially if the mother was not active or successful in a career herself.

If a woman chooses a dual career, including work inside as well as outside the home, the reality that will have to be faced both practically and emotionally is that of disrupted work. An obvious price to pay for discontinuity in professional work is the constraint on professional advancement. The combination of two careers strains a family situation and obviously requires, in order to be comfortable and acceptable, accommodation on the part of the husband (15). Unless negotiated, a husband's professional routines and personal life-style may be a constraint on the woman's participation in her own career.

The more a woman's sense of herself was grounded in her identity as a wife and a mother, the greater will be her readjustment in this respect when she enters the occupational world. Her sense of femaleness, attractiveness, and lovability will perhaps be seen as incompatible with being independent and just as competent as men.

Set against a background of cultural change, many of these issues may hitchhike on current or cultural events. Resentment of men may be claimed to be based on their chauvinism and prejudice, perhaps to a disproportionate degree. The husband or lover inherits the internal turmoil engendered in the woman's childhood. The mother may have failed her daughter by being an inadequate or unhappy model for identification. If the mother was poorly educated or housebound, she may simultaneously resent her own way of life and overtly defend it. She becomes envious of her daughter's aspirations to more freedom; the daughter intuitively senses this envy and is afraid to go ahead and be successful in a new way of her own, as it will mean giving up all hope of maternal approval or will cause the mother to have a depression. Such a mother may even have warned her daughter that a career would make it impossible to be either a good wife or a good mother; though the prediction can be consciously rejected, it can be an unconscious albatross.

Contemporary women between the ages of twenty-five and fifty face special problems in deciding their domestic, personal, and career roles. It may be hard for them to work out a stable life-style that allows the growth of their own interests and careers while still satisfying their needs to create a comfortable home atmosphere, raise children, and have a happy marriage. Since there is no universal or traditional precedent, it takes more than average self-esteem, ego strength, and clear sense of sexual identity to manage. Young children are bound to want Mother with them as much as possible, and both children and husband are apt to blame her when things do not go well. Other women may envy her or genuinely disagree with her arrangement, so that she often finds herself facing her dilemma alone. The husband who originally encouraged her to work outside the home, if that is the choice, may find himself later becoming unexpectedly demanding and may resent her turning her attention elsewhere. The husband may be ambivalent or perhaps more dependent on her than he knows, or even threatened by her competence. He may want her to outshine other women but not him, needing her to be dependent on him in ways that make him feel masculine and paternal. One problem for the woman who puts her efforts into being a totally dedicated mother, and who derives pride from this career, is that it is a transient one, lasting only a short number of years. The question then is, What do you do after that? Also, the culture in which we live gives esteem to successes other than mothering.

Since the dual role is more difficult, the woman who chooses it needs to be able to get real satisfaction from the variety and stimulation it offers, rather than feeling that special allowances should be made for her. If she got professional training to please an ambitious mother, or to be the son her father wanted, she may resent rather than enjoy it, expecting her husband to reward her for working so hard and earning her own money. He may enjoy having her do so providing she enjoys it also and does not take it out on him. This requires a degree of self-assurance and competence, a firm belief in one's ability to do well in both aspects of the dual role, which is very hard to achieve. Like many other types of rebels, women work against an entrenched system but simultaneously want partial approval from the old authorities (parents) and from their less-convinced co-workers (men). Neither of these groups may feel it has much to gain from change, so they are not likely to back it consistently.

"Equal" does not necessarily mean "identical." Without stereotypes, responsibilities are negotiable. Strenuous competition results from conflict of interest, individual preferences, and overlapping of dependency or narcissistic needs.

There may be obstacles for the individual who seeks achievement outside an accepted role. For the man, this may be to seek goals other than the expectable ones for him, both personally and professionally. For the woman who attempts significant accomplishment, there may be emotional pressures from society and from the individuals most important to her, including her own parents, husband, and children. The parents may not have had an emotional stake in their daughter's success as they had in that of a son; there is much less likelihood that there would have been significant sacrifices on the part of the parents to enable the daughter to pursue education and success.

Competency for some women may be allowed expression only in volunteerism. A woman, in volunteer work, may allow herself to be confident and competent with social congruency. As long as she strives and succeeds not for personal gain or independent financial reward but in a caring, concerned effort for others, her ideal of being a good woman is sustained. Energy and competence are applauded but not given financial compensation, one of the earmarks of success. Volunteer work may be a way to deal with the prohibition on entering the world of competition and power.

The woman who was raised to be pleasing, not assertive, giving to others even to the point of martyrdom, dependent, possibly timid, and centered on family has traditionally been considered to be better adapted to the task of mothering young children. Today the price of such character formations can be seen in the "empty-nest syndrome," when a woman of thirty-five or forty is no longer needed in the same way by her now-adolescent or older children and she faces another thirty or forty years without the goals that had been so significant until now.

One also has to wonder if what seems like such favorable mothering for young children is really such a fruitful adaptation, especially considering the model established for the young girl. Many women who wish to pursue work of their own are tormented by guilt, feeling that proper mother love does not permit the straying of attention. Others may suffer echoes of their own separation anxieties as children and hesitate to be away from their children lest something harmful befall them.

The concept of success changes depending on the time of the individual's life, as well as the culture and period in which she is living. In Hermann Hesse's novel *Siddhartha*, three stages in the pursuit of success are described. The first, coming in adolescence and early adulthood, comprises a successful separation from parents and survival in the wilderness. The second ("midlife") stage is pursuit of financial, business, and personal accomplishments. The final pursuit of success is in the simplicity of sitting on a riverbank and comfortably and happily listening to the music of the water.

The onset of middle age may be defined as the awareness of the illusion of timelessness and immortality. Midlife may be the time when previous choices in important life areas and the ensuing successes, failures, satisfactions, and disappointments are reviewed and reworked in the context of both new evidence and old aspirations and wishes. Recognition of the limitations in oneself, the finiteness of opportunity, and the irreversibility of time are extremely important emotional milestones. There is an inevitable midlife crisis of some degree when one recognizes that various wishes or goals are unfulfilled and others are unfulfillable. It can no longer be a question of "just a little more time" as one recognizes the finiteness of time and life itself. Thus there is some sort of mourning reaction to the recognition that one will never become a multimillionaire after all, or that one's husband will never undergo a metamorphosis into Robert Redford. There may be a disillusionment of sorts when one realizes the impossibility of achieving perfection, as reward and recognition on an ascending scale may level off.

CHAPTER 10

Success Inhibition

Definition

SUCCESS AND ACHIEVEMENT, in whatever context they are individually defined, are the fullest expression of the developmental thrust of mastery.* Mastery is a broad concept, referring to a functional synthesis of intrapsychic sublimation and organization with external goal-oriented tasks. The failure of any of the components of internal or external mastery, or of successfully and appropriately coupling the two, can result in failure of achievement.

Someone who has a success inhibition may work diligently while success or a completed achievement seems to be at a safe distance, but as the goal is approached, become anxious and sabotage efforts at successfully achieving that goal, or, just after achieving success, depreciate the achievement or the enjoyment of it.

---

*I would even postulate a developmental line of work, spawned from the desire for mastery, manifested first in childhood play and later in adult work. This hypothesis awaits further exploration.

Anxiety and ambivalence may then result in renunciation of the goal or denial of the recognition of success. Or detachment, depressive symptoms, depersonalization, or psychosomatic symptoms may become manifest.

Why would someone fall ill emotionally or physically, or sabotage her efforts, just when a long-sought-for goal is imminent or has been achieved? "So much the more surprising, indeed bewildering, must it appear when as a physician one makes the discovery that people fall ill precisely because a deeply rooted and long-cherished wish has come to fulfillment" (1). This observation by Freud recognized the unconscious forces that induce illness when success is obtained. It is as if "one is never more on trial than in the moment of excessive good fortune" (2).

It is necessary to provide some backdrop against which to view and understand the aspects of intrapsychic development, conflict, and compromise formation to understand success inhibition. The various manifestations of success inhibition will then be explored, and developmental origins of these manifestations will be examined.

Anxiety is a psychological event which can be developmentally defined as the response to a traumatic situation or danger, present or anticipated. A *danger* situation is one in which helplessness is anticipated, whereas a *traumatic* situation is one in which helplessness occurs or is experienced. *Neurotic anxiety* is a reaction which is currently disproportionate to objective danger and involves intrapsychic conflict. Symptoms may be manifested as tremulousness, tension, or even psychosomatic ailments like diarrhea or stomach cramps. Anxiety may be the feeling that "something bad" is going to happen. The "something bad" will have different meanings for each person, consistent with that person's ideational content and developmental history.

A *phobia* is a specific defense against anxiety in which a function is inhibited or a perceived danger situation is avoided. The danger is symbolically projected or displaced onto an external object or situation, and this object or situation is avoided. The phobic idea or thought is basically a mental representation of intimidation or a fear of violence toward oneself. The phobia is a stand-in, a representative, for something one is frightened of, something beyond one's awareness, which is unconscious. A *suc-*

cessful defense may amount to a *failure in achievement.* An inhibition of achievement may not be recognized for the intrapsychic conflict which it is. Additionally, "success phobia" may exist in women without any other notable or apparent evidence of psychopathology. There may even be a history of relatively well-adjusted and conflict-free relationships.

The Various Manifestations

While it would seem that a success phobia would be easily recognized, some of the various manifestations will be reviewed, as they may go unrecognized. The manifestations represent a final common denominator of various developmental difficulties for different individuals; thus, there is no consistently generalizable coupling of a certain manifestation of success phobia with a specific underlying pathology.

Inhibition of achievement may be encountered in numerous areas: vocational, academic, maternal, marital, and sexual, to name a few. A crucial clinical issue is the recognition of the various ways in which the fear of achievement and ambition present. Some of the more common manifestations will be reviewed: avoidance of a final step toward success, erosion of successful accomplishment, and ambition without goal-setting. Further illustrations will then be given in the section on developmental origins.

AVOIDANCE OF THE FINAL STEP

The final step of successful accomplishment may be phobically avoided. Anxiety may reach a crescendo just before the culmination of a task, only to be calmed by a withdrawal from the final completion. The graduate student may literally lack a few lines on the last paragraph of her Ph.D. dissertation and decide to abandon it, or she may become an interminable or perpetual student, and thereby postpone success. She may fear to be discovered as a "phony" when taking her final doctoral examinations. She may plan more than she can possibly achieve, forestalling completion and success.

The path to success may be barred early, before success can possibly be achieved. The student may forget to register or to

take an entrance exam. A job applicant may come late or antagonize her interviewer. The fear of success may also be whispered
in the everyday "choke" or "clutch": becoming anxious on examinations, for example, or being unable to polish off an opponent
at tennis. Someone clearly in the lead may falter when winning is
imminent. Progress in resolving these conflicts can often be in-
dexed by the course of change in a person's game. One woman
described tennis as the only time where she could comfortably
express herself and be aggressive. It had become, for her, a circumscribed area within which she granted herself permission to
vent otherwise isolated assertive and aggressive feelings. She
added, "I also choke when I'm ahead. I lose concentration at
those times. I do best when I'm on automatic and don't think
about winning—it's like I'm faking myself out."

Major developmental achievements, such as taking an important position, getting promoted, graduating, or even getting
married may often be sabotaged at the final step. Most often
these conflicts represent unconscious issues, which are incom-
prehensible to the woman intellectually. That these issues are
unconscious, emotional, and often consciously illogical explains
why she finds self-help books or intellectual explanations frus-
tratingly inadequate.

As long as there is no appreciable success, she can work
toward a goal fervently and relatively unambivalently. If and
when the success becomes imminent, anxiety manifests itself
and the near-success is replaced with a mandate to avoid it. She
functions well as long as her goals remain distant, but when success and completion are approached, progress is halted or di-
verted. Anxiety, rather than propelling an individual toward a
better performance, may do just the opposite. For example, one
student who entered an exam suffered mental confusion and hys-
terical paralysis of her writing hand; she could not complete the
exam.

The perception of this conflict by the woman may involve seeing it as a fear of failing, a fear of rejection or humiliation. Feeling herself to be the object of criticism or inadequate to live up
to expectations, she may then abandon a long-cherished goal and
perhaps substitute alternate goals. One woman indicated that
she had never reached her full capacity because she had never
stayed with a company as consultant for more than eighteen
months. She indicated that as soon as she was at a job for twelve

to eighteen months, she began feeling anxiety because people around her had seen her total expertise and she no longer had anything to teach them. She would then begin to feel that she was the subject of criticism and increased scrutiny, since she was not absolutely certain that she knew more than anyone working with her. Her failure to internally acknowledge her expertise propelled her to continually avoid anticipated exposure of inadequacy.

A related type of inhibition exists in the person who can never allow herself to function at fullest capacity. A fear of criticism or of failing results in a built-in protection with the implicit assumption, "If I had really given it my all, I would have succeeded." The fear of making a mistake may create an inhibition or restraint, based on the expectation of criticism for any performance less than perfect.

Completion of successful endeavors is difficult for the narcissistic individual who has required constant or immediate feedback or applause. Sustained effort without external admiration on an ongoing basis is often stalled.

A characterological resolution to this conflict about success may be the belief that staying in the background guarantees safety and will not reveal supposed weaknesses and inadequacies. The fear of being discovered to be an imposter or of having "bluffed one's way along" is a common element in success phobia. The person reasons that with greater success will come a potentially harder fall. Being viewed by others as highly competent often is coupled with the internal feeling of being incompetent, inadequate, or an imposter. The rationalized lowering of one's ambition is the stepping back from the anxiety-provoking success situations. With this step backward a depression may develop, the reaction to the loss reverberating with the loss of self-esteem.

EROSION OF SUCCESSFUL ACCOMPLISHMENT

There are well-known characters in literature who surprisingly fall ill precisely because a deeply rooted wish comes to fulfillment, as though they could not endure their success. Shakespeare's Lady Macbeth and Ibsen's Rebecca West had grave illnesses almost immediately following the knowledge that a major wish fulfillment was actually at hand, and thus they destroyed all enjoyment of their success. The success-fearing woman can work diligently toward success and completion when it is at a safe distance, but becomes anxious and sabotages her performance as success is approached, or falls ill or otherwise destroys the products of her efforts immediately after the recognition of success.

Self-defeating behavior may erode performance, motivation, or completion. Money, prestige, or achievement may be destroyed or depreciated. This sabotage of work-related efforts may manifest in efforts to sabotage work itself: making errors, having accidents, being chronically late, or always procrastinating. A self-defeating attitude is exemplified by the patient who stated, "Whenever I do something really well and someone acknowledges or compliments me, I have to point out something that is not good—a criticism or flaw. It has the quality of undoing whatever I do." Another woman stated, "If I get a compliment about how I look, I think to myself, 'Well, if you saw me without my makeup, you wouldn't think I was so pretty.'" Whenever she looked in the mirror, rather than seeing a model's face which was professionally photographed for cosmetics ads, she focused entirely on her one "flaw"—an almost imperceptible freckle. Her feelings about herself were negative, despite ample contrary evidence. She disallowed any intimate relationships because she feared that eventually she would be rejected when someone found out what she was really like. Presupposing an eventual rejection, she engineered many.

A promotion or advancement may be met with depression or anxiety, which may be disruptive enough to prevent maximum or adequate functioning and cause lack of fulfillment of a goal. A major depression in response to a significant corporate advancement has been experienced by some women. Other reactions, involving on the surface a move away from traditional feminine patterns, may not be so deeply rooted or profound as success neurosis based on significant internal conflicts.

Symptoms of anxiety may often arise at times of successful intellectual activity. Headaches may occur. Concentration may become confused and blurred. The person may find it difficult to maintain stamina after successful completion of an endeavor. Ideas may become muddled and imprecise. Inhibitions may then occur in business or professional functioning.

Often patients seek treatment at times of major transition, such as graduation from college. One way to avoid this crisis is to remain a perpetual student, accumulating degrees, or almost accumulating a number of degrees but remaining in a student status. One student I knew was on her sixth "major" in as many years. Their situation is perplexing to these students because they consciously want success in school and other endeavors, but feel inadequate, undeserving, or unable to firmly realize or understand their prohibitions to achievement.

A number of women already established in a career who suffer from work inhibition feel a sense of being an imposter, as if something critically needed in them is missing (3). Furthermore, these women express the idea that rather than having progressed on the basis of skill and accomplishment, one is "born to do something." Most of these women have not been able to enjoy their success. They are afraid of becoming too powerful and ultimately sadistic in their competitiveness. Many of their problems related to aggression involve conflict about surpassing a mother who is seen to be weak and "only a woman." The basic self-esteem of these career women is problematic, as they have deeply-rooted convictions of inferiority.

Success is downplayed with one of several defensive maneuvers. Accomplishments may be disavowed, attributed to "accident," "luck," or "circumstances" rather than to motivation and work. The woman may convince herself that she has fooled anyone who feels she is really intelligent. One woman felt that she was mistakenly admitted to medical school because of an error by the admissions committee.

A unique way of redefining and perceiving success is the declaration of an accomplishment as a failure in order to be able to proceed. When a woman actually does accomplish something, she may disguise or camouflage it to the extent that its appearance goes unheralded. If one expects to be zapped (abandoned, criticized, incapable to make it alone, etc.) as the finish line is crossed, then it had better be avoided, or at least not perceived as the finish line. One woman accepted the successful completion of specialty and subspecialty training as well as the successful completion of psychotherapeutic treatment by initially referring to them as failures; other completions in the past had been accepted, amid much anxiety, if they were likewise denigrated. These perceived "failures" confirmed and enhanced the woman's sense of inadequacy. This woman focused on her difficult marriage, her decision of choosing between husband and lover, and the decision of where to open her practice, diverting attention from the substantial accomplishment of completion of years of professional training and completion of treatment. More specifically, her emotional dilemmas were viewed as a "chronic illness" for which there was no hope of cure. In this case, the patient's mother had a chronic illness—multiple sclerosis—so the cure of the patient's illness and the termination of her treatment were seen as surpassing the mother, who had no hope of definitive treatment or cure. The mother was also surpassed in another way: upon the completion of professional training, the patient had now concretely achieved more than her nonprofessional mother. These accomplishments had been unconsciously equated with an Oedipal victory, made more feasible as a child when she and her father shared many activities together, excluding the mother because of her illness.

The sense of guilt over an achievement (or even a wish for achievement) may be displaced onto a woman's family. Her constricting superego is thrust onto her family or husband, who is then seen as the source of impediment of significant movement. Often the cast of characters has been chosen so that they are prepared to and often do play their parts well. For example, the woman who has an unconscious inhibition of achievement is often married to a man who, reciprocally, has ambivalence about his wife achieving and being successful. The system and patterns within the original family may be replicated in this manner.

A fear of failure is the opposite side of the same coin: it is a rationalized fear of success, made consciously understandable. Almost every person whom I have seen with some form of success inhibition has tried to explain (to herself) her difficulty on this basis. The consequence is the same: to avoid completion of an effort, to retreat from competition and divert success, or, upon successful completion of a task, to withdraw, depreciate, or erode the accomplishment. The diversion from success may give the appearance of indolence or laziness.

AMBITION WITHOUT GOAL-SETTING

One way persons may avoid success is by not setting goals or by establishing goals that are vague or undefined. This insures that goals will never be reached, thereby avoiding the assumed consequences of success. A person may use a belief in luck and destiny to disavow pursuit of goal-directed behavior and accomplishment. A patient stated, "If I do something well it's because of luck or it just happening, and if I fail at something, it's my fault." This dilemma characterizes the perplexity caused by an internal impediment to success. A belief in predetermination, fate, or God's will may be the rationalized disavowal of one's own effort in achievement. This veil over responsibility for one's efforts and goals disallows recognition of accomplishment and the full enjoyment of mastery.

An alternate way of handling this issue is to set more goals than one can possibly accomplish, thus insuring that none will be reached or successfully completed.

Often ambitious feelings can be very intense, yet coupled with passively achieved goals. Even when achieving, for example, a highly specialized or technical degree and skill, one may hope to be pursued and "discovered" by an employer in order to receive the perfect position. After obtaining a specialized degree in the science field, one young woman told of her fantasy that potential employers would find out about her skills and accomplishments and tailor-make a job just for her. Her failure to take realistic steps to acquaint potential employers with her expertise left her disappointed when nothing happened. This combination of ambition coupled with passivity is an example of how ambition can be unfulfilled when the conscious and unconscious goals oppose one another. Grandiose goals and expectations of achievement, even a sense of entitlement that one achieve, reflect the magical thinking of early childhood in which one becomes a princess overnight, movie stars are discovered at the corner drugstore, and the four-year-old is thrust into a bases-loaded, bottom-of-the-ninth batting position to hit a home run and win the series.

A woman may feel as if she suddenly needs to become ambitious and to work or have a career, needing to support herself economically or become a more well-rounded individual. This sudden desire, as opposed to a long-term ambition or passionate interest to succeed, may create its own problem. An imperative which is sudden or externally determined creates difficulty, since motivation may not be as intense or as well planned as if this goal had been lifelong. The woman who has made her goal since childhood that of developing interpersonal relationships, social skills, and domestic interests may find difficulty in suddenly switching goals as well as ambition. One's life work is more complicated than this, exemplified by many successful careers which can be traced to early interests going back to childhood. The magical promise of fulfillment through work becomes elusive and disappointing and may result in a renewed sense of failure.

Developmental Origins

While anxiety will drive and motivate toward achievement at some levels, at higher levels it will cause the achievement motivation to become derailed and subverted. The problem, of course, is not simply the level of anxiety but the specificity of anxiety and its unconscious equations.

An important question in looking at internal conflict is that of developmental diagnosis. Developmental diagnosis asks the question: Where in developmental time is the nucleus of the current struggle or conflict? It is imperative as a therapist to understand the developmental issues with which the patient is struggling in order to be able to empathically understand the level, intensity, and content of conflicts which preclude realizing one's full potential. That potential may be for internal comfort, happiness, relatedness with others, sense of self, or successful achievement. For a women who fears success to the point of erosion of accomplishments, self-destructive efforts, or avoidance of initiating autonomous endeavors, the explanation is much deeper and more complex than simply a fear of being seen as unattractive, ineligible, and unfeminine if she is successful.

Some of the major lines of development will be discussed below, as pathology in these areas gives rise to success inhibition. The therapeutic issues will be discussed in Chapter 12.

SEPARATION–INDIVIDUATION ORIGINS

The women with earliest developmental conflict unconsciously equate success with creating a breach in a dyadic bond with the mother. An anticipation of retaliation from the mother in earliest childhood becomes a fear of severance in the relationship and of abandonment by her. With women whose conflicts are in this developmental area, success (meaning autonomy and independence) reverberates with the first sense of autonomy and independence in the separation–individuation phase between two and three years of age. If there have been difficulties with this phase of development, there is extreme anxiety associated with steps toward autonomy, the loss of the child's belief in her omnipotence, and concern about the emotional availability of the parents (4).

Following an episode of success, a woman may feel depressed and depleted, and retreat into a withdrawn state. The excitement stimulated by the success may be followed by a feeling of depletion and ennui. Success is unconsciously equated at one level with the withdrawal of the continuing and consistent input of the mother, who leaves if success and autonomy are effected. Historically, the mother, unable to accept the loss, dissuades her daughter from separation by abandoning her emotionally when the daughter takes a step toward self-sufficiency. When the resultant state of aloneness and abandonment is experienced, a rapprochement with the mother is effected, and the mother is once more warm and responsive. There is, in addition, a fear of becoming angry, which would destroy the continuity that is experienced, since it poses an even greater threat of the retaliatory abandonment of the mother.

A girl at the age of two or three experiences envy of the perceived omnipotence of her mother, feeling weak and impotent by contrast, and fearing that she cannot achieve the success and autonomy she desires unless the mother is present emotionally and physically, repairing magically severed bonds experienced by the girl (5). In wishing to be endowed with omnipotence, the girl of two or three wishes to magically possess what her mother has, and wants to change places with the mother, an anlage of identification. This wish to exchange places with the mother, if realized, would render the mother as impotent as the girl feels, resulting in a reversal of roles and victory over the mother. This unconscious fantasy that power and success would be achieved at the expense of the mother induces unconscious guilt, and lies at the origin of guilt experienced as an adult when success is viewed as defeating and hurting someone else, especially a woman. For the girl of two or three, robbing her mother of her power would mean that each of the girl's successes would be equated with a painful loss or failure for the mother (5).

A type of success phobia is seen in those persons whose parents disallowed appropriate separation and autonomy during development. Parents may communicate subtle messages to the child that she is not able to do things herself. The parents of success-fearing children make substantially more critical comments, give more hints and commands, and make more attempts to do tasks for the child than the parents of non-success-fearing children. The child may also interpret the parents' active participation as more valuable than her own—an indication that the parents do not want her to act independently. The child may finally conclude that she is incapable of doing tasks alone. She may be sick on days at school when competitions or examinations are being held. Such views of oneself are internalized and become woven into the fabric of character structure. This structure then influences behavior in various ways: to remain silent when holding an opposing viewpoint, to fear that one cannot present herself well or be considered intelligent in expressing oneself, to use charm and perceptiveness to win the approval of others. This process of seeking and gaining the approval of admired others is unsuccessful in changing internal views about oneself, since the responses are based on attributes other than intellect or accomplishment. The other people may be simply discounted as unable to judge the girl accurately, perpetuating the dichotomy of the true self and the facade.

A common feature in the developmental history of the phobic personality is a parent or parents who do not foster the child's attempts at achieving mastery. The parents themselves in many instances have phobias which are transmitted as fearful attitudes to the developing child (6, 7). Overprotectiveness not only shields the child from hardship but disallows learning to persevere in the face of adversity. Parents can, in extreme cases, subject attempts at mastery and acquisition of skills to criticism and belittlement and thus cripple the crucial development of mastery and self-expression. The environment then becomes a source of terror. Adult phobic anxiety in the phobic personality will be a constant struggle. Being afraid of various aspects of living or of various encounters—e.g., being afraid to drive, to fly, to swim, or to succeed at vocational or professional endeavors—may create such a need for adjustment and detour around them that much of the joy of living is bypassed.

Phobic responses are multidetermined. One aspect may be a hangover from an earlier failure to achieve mastery in childhood and thus be motivated by an unresolved dependency need. Parents may have had an active hand in determining the specificity of the phobia. Another facet may involve a fear of losing control over sexual impulses, with a withdrawal to a dependent and safer position. In these instances the anxiety is not related to independence but stems indirectly from the repressed sexual impulses. Somatic manifestations of anxiety such as palpitations, dizziness, shortness of breath, and faintness are the manifest focus of phobic persons. The magical yet understandable wish for a medical focus and treatment of these symptoms serves an anxiety-containing function. Anxiety is converted or channeled into somatic expression.

As an adult, each new increment of independent functioning harbors the fear of loss of an important person, unconsciously reverberating with a perception that success and autonomy are achieved at the expense of the mother. Any achievement or significant endeavor becomes unconsciously perceived as hurting or destroying a rival. The only safe consequence of this internal struggle and equation is to inhibit aggression and assertion. Since any achievement and any success-seeking endeavor represent some derivative of a severance of the bond with a necessary pre-Oedipal mother, efforts at this kind of independence and achievement are usually abandoned before an outright success, thus allaying a feared abandonment and loss with its concomitant depression.

A difficulty in working arising from separation anxiety is illustrated by an attorney who could not concentrate on work at her office desk except for very short periods of time. She would quickly become distracted and restless, and need to have contact with someone else. The isolation created by her concentration had to be interrupted by "connecting" herself with someone: her secretary, a telephone caller, or just someone she greeted as she walked around the floor of her building. A promotion to partnership precipitated major anxiety episodes as she perceived losing her former security, dependence, and peers.

ORIGINS IN PATHOLOGICAL NARCISSISM

A particular type of work inhibition is produced in someone with narcissistic tendencies who is preoccupied with the risk of failure or even the risk of making a mistake. Any type of performance ushers in the possibility of making a mistake, which is equated with the person's being flawed. Situations are avoided in which the person does not have certainty that she can succeed—and succeed from the very outset. Along with unrealistically high expectations and ambitions is the simultaneous self-reproach, sometimes bitter, for failing to live up to these standards. Ambitions may be pursued up to a certain point, only for the person to withdraw just before the moment of real testing. She may withdraw an application to a prestigious school just before being "turned down," or fail to complete papers or dissertations, or manage not to take her examinations. Most often, a sudden and puzzling disappearance of interest occurs in what had seemed to be a most engrossing pursuit.

The interest of such individuals in the chosen endeavors seems to be characterized more by ideas of some narcissistic gain—having an illustrious career or being admired—than by the satisfaction of functioning in the job itself. They therefore view their difficulties as evidence of some grievous basic defect in their makeup which they feel powerless to remedy. They may also resent any discomfort, including the discomforts of experiencing difficulties in a task, and respond with rage and the feeling that something unfair is occurring. This particularly undermines their motivation for attempting to surmount their difficulties, because they feel more or less consciously that they should not be expected to put up with such problems. They therefore appeal to fate, await outside intervention, or attempt to discover tricks that will make the difficulty disappear. When magic is not invoked, and when others do not respond in exactly the desired way (which is to function as an extension of the individual—as if there were two bodies with one head), a narcissistic rage may follow.

The individual may come to treatment with a picture of general doubt about her capacity, even to the point of conviction that some central feature necessary for success is missing and that in academic life or in work she has fooled people or gained her position fraudulently. She may feel that she can attain her ends only through some special manipulations, through capitalizing on her "weakness." She experiences a strong sense of having been deprived or injured, and insists upon redress of her grievances. Her expressed admiration of men, even to the point of worship, is a desperate attempt to not allow into consciousness the envy and rage which necessitate the veneer of their opposites. This feeling seems to be related to the attribution by these women, together with the rest of society, of a "masculine" character to achievement, especially in certain fields such as science and medicine.

There are many strategies which will enable the success-fearing woman both to satisfy lofty ambitions and to keep herself in check. When progressing well, she is likely to belittle herself and thus to create in her imagination a great chasm between herself and her competitors. Holding a low opinion of herself and her abilities, she can allay anxiety about succeeding while still progressing. Rejecting favorable information as flattery or chance, she is likely to attribute her accomplishments to luck, to other people, or to virtually any factor that will allow her to maintain a perception that she is in no way a real success. This is like having to feed a two-headed animal, with both heads requiring equal fare. One head demands ambition and recognition of accomplishment; the other demands active disclaimers of any perceptions of accomplishment. As one gains more, the other must keep pace to maintain the equilibrium. Although the person is outwardly self-denigrating, an active fantasy life often involves grand ambition. These secret fantasies originate from childhood efforts to repair wounded self-esteem.

Sometimes a woman enters marriage with the expectation that her husband and especially her children will fill a need for self-validation. Her admiration of the husband's competence and her vicarious identification with his success is not enough for these deep emotional needs. She may fear that her vitality is unfeminine as well as a possible threat to her husband, thereby eclipsing her potential to a secondary position or ancillary role. The reciprocal of the fear of success in the woman may be the husband's ambivalence about her success. Someone may then be sought out who will recognize, validate, and even foster her ambition. By being more empathically in tune with herself, she may then be able to sustain her own growth. The function of another person validating and accepting her ambition may be served in various women by a mentor, husband, close friend, national figure, or therapist.

Various ways these concerns may manifest include a decision between career and marriage, between a career and motherhood, or some other compromise fashioned out of respect to an unconscious dilemma. The woman may allow herself a career only as long as she functions as a subordinate, never accepting the emotionally risky position of autonomy and concomitant responsibility. Coping may mean receiving benevolent approval from whoever is endowed with and perceived to have power. An eventual rebellion occurs against this self-imposed bondage, usually precipitated by a narcissistic injury such as insufficient valuation of the woman's loyalty and devotion, whereupon there is hurt and its rapid successor, anger. When her obsequious behavior does not pay off by creating the response that would be given to a special child, anger ensues. The woman is now in a curious bind: she is not being treated like a favorite child, nor has success been sanctioned.

Feeling cheated in life, as though she were deprived by her mother of something which others have and which she needs in order to feel whole and potent, may be translated as "penis envy." A masochistic character structure in such a woman is not uncommon, with the basic mechanism being aggressiveness and anger at her mother turned toward herself and the wish for revenge on the mother occurring most intensely at times of success, thus manifesting as masochistic sabotage at the very time of success.

OEDIPAL ORIGINS

When enmeshed in Oedipal conflict, the thrill of victory and success assumes the defeat of an opponent. One woman attorney put it most succinctly: "Childhood seemed like a series of win-or-lose situations. It always seemed that if I would win, someone else would lose or suffer. It wasn't necessarily physical warfare, but a series of win-or-lose situations or bitter sarcasm to reduce myself or others to tears. I realize that when I win in a legal situation in court now, I feel bad and pity the opponent." Thus the thrill of success is leavened by an imagined opponent's agony of defeat. A legitimate arena for the enactment of this conflict was found in the woman's choice of a legal career.

A seed is planted in childhood for a particular view of competitiveness and work with other women. This seed—the Oedipal situation—is present in everyone. However, only in a certain soil and climate will it grow to become a conflictual issue and express itself in work inhibition. The conditions may be provided by the mother, who is herself actually competitive with her daughter, having been threatened by the daughter's capability, attractiveness, or expressiveness; or the father may respond in a somewhat seductive manner, making the actualization of the wish to attract him too dangerously close, necessitating an anxiety-laden retreat. The father may feel competitive himself, if his sense of manliness is threatened by the emerging competence of his young daughter. Alienation between parents such that the child can win the parent of the opposite sex away from the other parent by taking sides intensifies the Oedipal dilemma. This situation may arise when one or both parents are narcissistic, when attempts at individuation are stifled by parents, or when a parent is psychologically or physically absent, such as in the case of parent loss by death, divorce, or prolonged separation. Physical intimidation from either parents or siblings reinforces the unconscious equation between success, on one side, and aggression, on the other. The desire, usually unconscious, for victory over a powerful rival or intimidator generates both guilt and the fear of an equally violent retaliation. The result is an inhibition or withholding of aggression. The inhibition of aggression is then extended in application to assertion in general (8). Or, if success is achieved, guilt may require suffering or some penance, thus initiating masochistic or self-sabotaging efforts. A further step in the generalization of this conflict is that any subsequent competition, identified unconsciously with the original rivalry of childhood, is inhibited.

The compromise-formation of this conflict is in some ways adaptive for the child. If physical intimidation by parents or siblings becomes a reality, inhibition of aggression is even more important. An atmosphere of violence or hostile competition results in the anticipation of attack or retaliation by others. Of course this inhibition of aggression undermines self-confidence, esteem, and effectiveness, and may result in the chronic sense of inadequacy. If intimidating or abusive behavior by parents becomes a reality in the sense of an actual retaliation, then the unconscious assumption becomes a reality. The reality assumes the characteristics of a traumatic neurosis, with the child experiencing weakness and helplessness.

Assertion becomes unconsciously equated with success, and may be defended by a passivity in which the object of success-striving is abandoned, distorted, or substituted. The basic wish is not to fail, but failing before a final step of success may be equated unconsciously with the position of passivity and safety, thus sparing oneself the dangerous consequences of self-assertion. The central conflict is the fear to be and act as a full-fledged woman, because the powerful parent of the same sex is seen as a prohibitive and threatening force who would not approve of incestuous erotic feelings and would punish their expression. The later adult derivative, success-related anxiety, may entail expectation of catastrophe as a product of efforts at self-assertion. The final step or passageway to the successful completion of a task then evokes the manifestation of anxiety by strong unconscious forces, and anxiety ultimately gains ascendancy. Fear and guilt are thus incurred not because of inferior ability but because of an assumption that superior performance would result in a taboo victory. Performance must then be either sabotaged directly or depreciated by a perception of inconsequence if the performance is completed. The failure becomes the rationalized consequence. The problem is not innate inability, but an inhibition by fear, since success is unconsciously perceived as aggressive and competitive. A whisper of this fear of success is difficulty accepting compliments without embarrassment or comments depreciating either the outcome or the significance of performance. The ambivalence about achievement and success are captured in one woman's words after a particularly noteworthy accomplishment: "I'm amazed—I just felt like I didn't have it. Sometimes I wish I didn't."

When competitive feelings emerge in the girl, the mother is seen as a rival while at the same time remaining a loved, respected, and necessary person, from whom continuing love is sought. If the competition were to be pursued so that the young girl would become accepted by the father when she won, this would antagonize the powerful mother. Above all, the girl fears that her mother would retaliate by withdrawing her nurturance and support. The fear of angry abandonment by the mother makes it seem necessary to conceal her competitive wishes, as any arena in which they might be portrayed could be fraught with anxiety. The fear culminates in a protective self-imposed defeat.

The girl who cannot succeed because it involves for her the winning of an incestuous battle with Mother for Father's exclusive attention will be quite different from the girl whose insecure mother needs others to confirm and validate her own sense of worth. This neediness by the mother leaves the child in a position of insecurity and fragility. This girl might develop into a woman who feels herself not as a separate person, but as a devitalized one, whose goals, competence, and sense of direction in life need the mirroring approvement of someone else. These borrowed goals and directions further erode the sense of self.

An intrinsic resolution of dealing with aggression, if aggression does not fit one's ideal or is enmeshed with conflict, is to defend against the aggression by seeing oneself as inadequate. This defensive position becomes a basic assumption which is then enacted to confirm and validate a supposed sense of inadequacy. A woman with this type of conflict lives constantly with a sense of guilt. Her superego does not tolerate aggression or its expression, and redirects it back on herself, making her feel guilty for the hostility. The guilt, in turn, makes her feel inadequate, as her superego constantly berates her for this hostility. Hostility is then enhanced by unfulfilled abilities, intellectual potentials, interests, and ambitions.

For some women who have anxiety in the face of success, the provocateur is competition rather than success per se. The anxiety of competition may create a restructuring, internally or externally, so that competition is not present or is camouflaged. When a fear is externalized (fear of work, for example) the internal conflict from which the fear arises remains untouched. The concern about competition may involve concerns about disapproval, surpassing others, loss of dependency, and fear of retaliation.

A common perception of the assertiveness often required for successful achievement is that each time one person succeeds another fails or is beaten. This may be the predominant conflict for some women, since a major component of a woman's ideal is that of being caring and giving to others: the core identification with her own mother. In fact, some of the most successful women are those whose mothers were not caring and giving in this way. Identification with a mother who was not nurturing and "maternal" has been a major factor in their compulsive drive for success and achievement, based on a compensatory identification with the father, toward whom they turned as children at the time of maternal empathic failure.

One retreat from a fear of success is to be submissive and deferential to a man. The use of charm and sex appeal, rather than competence, is seen to be the primary factor in achievement. Avoidance of competition with men or women is another such compromise.

Intense sibling rivalry may enhance conflicts about competition. If a child believes that her parents accord greater love and esteem to a brother or sister, then the child is likely to feel intense competition toward the preferred sibling. This intense rivalry leads to strong impulses to vanquish the preferred sibling and to usurp the more favorable position with the parents. As in the Oedipal conflict, fear of retaliation from the sibling and punishment from the parents leads to guilt, inhibition of competition, and repression of anger.

A promotion involving money, status, or other success may be unconsciously tantamount to an Oedipal victory. If this current success is heir to significant unresolved Oedipal conflict, the unwelcome accompanying benefactors may include guilt about competence and a fear of retaliation ("losing everything I've gained"; "paying for it in other ways") or of abandonment ("being envied but all alone with my success"). To insure safety from such unconscious expectations, the desired goal may be relinquished. Accompanying that surrender, a self-image of competence and assuredness may be eroded.

An example of psychosomatic manifestation of a particular type of success fear is pseudocyesis, or false pregnancy. The physical sensations and condition of pregnancy are replicated to the extent that in one case a woman was brought into the delivery room fully extended, dilated, and in full "labor" at nine months only to surprise herself and her doctor when her pregnancy turned out to be an emotional rather than a physical reality. Pseudocyesis represents a compromise-formation involving ambivalent desire for and fear of pregnancy. The unconscious motivation may be based on the wish to have a baby combined with the taboo against so doing. A wish and fear are wrapped in one "as if" package: pregnancy without a baby. The woman who cannot get her own consent for complete sexuality is another such example of a wish perceived as taboo: the permission for sexual behavior leading to orgasmic pleasure is inhibited.

Folklore provides a retrospective view of the concurrence of guilt and achievement in women. The ambitious woman is punished in folklore if she forges ahead and glories in her own achievement. She may be made infertile, and be unable to bear children, or fear that her children will be sick or incompetent if she is too ambitious. The counterpart in a man of this punishment for inappropriate ambition is that his infertility would be assured by an occurrence affecting his reproductive organ.

Competition, Aggression, and Femininity

The woman who feels that her career activities are masculine may have concern that she will lose her sexual identity as a woman, including her attractiveness to men. She may subsequently shrink from similar attempts and generally limit her horizons. Margaret Mead has noted that a woman's femininity seems to be called into question by her success.

One extremely capable and successful businesswoman struggled constantly to avoid the awareness that she was more active, energetic, and capable than her husband. She was afraid that she would damage him through her very capability, and as a result struggled to inhibit her expansiveness and limit the horizons of her ambition. She had grown up a favorite of an unsuccessful father who had been nagged and criticized by the mother, and the mother was at the same time apparently jealous of the daughter's successes. The patient resolved not to repeat this pattern. She married a man she considered the opposite of her father, only to have it turn out, as is so often the case, that he was essentially the same.

Another emotional factor for the career-oriented woman to contend with is the reaction of her peers and her fear that they may withdraw their support. Reactions to an interest other than the norm of a peer group may range from a lack of peer support to openly negative reactions toward those who are succeeding or successful. The women's movement has not eliminated this tragic conflict. Many outstanding women have experienced depreciation and attack from other women along with their success. In an article in *Ms.* Magazine entitled "Trashing: The Dark Side of Sisterhood," Joreen describes the painful disillusionment of her experience with other women's reactions to women's achievement (9). She states:

> Trashing is a particularly vicious form of character assassination which has reached epidemic proportions in the women's liberation movement . . . to disparage, destroy and ultimately exclude certain women.
>
> Achievement or accomplishment of any kind seems to be the worst crime. If you are assertive—if you do not fit the stereotype of feminine woman—it's all over . . . the values of the Movement favor women who are self-effacing. . . . Women exhibiting potential for achievement are punished by both women and men.

A form of work inhibition is the seeming inability to complete a task and live up to a promise, or the more active position of bringing about a destructive turn of events. Assuming that criticism is "in the air" and will be forthcoming regardless, perhaps in an unexpected and inconsistent way, the individual provokes criticism in some manner in order to at least be in control of it when it comes. Merely being at work or engaging in an endeavor is perceived as a form of exposure, creating vulnerability and inevitable criticism or danger.

Presupposing that an endeavor will be rejected, criticized, or ridiculed, one may assume the function of a critical editor and reject first, which not only insures the feared and hurtful rejection but may even preclude attempting the endeavor. In this internal scenario, the "critical other" is one's own superego, looking upon one's affects and motivation harshly and as a supposed transgression. The conclusion often erroneously reached is that one must be incapable or "second-rate," or the endeavor would have been completed comfortably.

Fearing rejection, the woman may not do her best, assuming that if she does her best and fails, the hurt will be even more devastating. An analogy is the college student who, upon beginning a test, declares that she has not really studied very much. If she does well, then it is *lagniappe*. If total effort were expended, and she failed, she would be embarrassed by the result. A dilemma inherent in this self-protective reasoning is that it does not allow 100 percent effort and thus may bring about what is feared the most.

Spontaneity, creativity, and originality are areas especially susceptible to inhibition and restraint. Successes may be averted if they are viewed as thrusting one in the limelight, since that focus of attention may carry with it the expectation of being in the harsh light of criticism. The assumption is made that one will not be accepted or will be criticized. Given this expectation, it is seemingly preferable to "beat the gun" and criticize oneself or to be in control of the criticism by doing something which one is certain will evoke a critical response. One may simply be unable to accept compliments without deprecatory or disavowing comments or, alternately, be driven to continuously seek approval to counterbalance an unconscious disapproval of inner affects or motives.

The attitudes toward women who succeed were cleverly listed in a study by Horner (10) in which she had men and women at a large coeducational university complete the two cues:

1. "After first-term finals, Anne finds herself at the top of her medical school class."
2. "After first-term finals, John finds himself at the top of his medical school class."

The responses from the girls were grouped into three categories:

1. Fear of social rejection.
2. Concern about one's normality or femininity.
3. Denial of the cue.

Girls in the latter category showed remarkable ingenuity in denying the cue. Responses included: "Anne is a code name for a nonexistent person created by a group of med students. They take turns taking exams and writing papers for her." "Anne is talking to her counselor. The counselor says she will make a fine nurse. She will continue her med school courses. She will study very hard and find she can and will become a good nurse." More than 70 percent of the respondents described Anne as being physically unattractive and having "lonely Friday and Saturday nights." She was specifically described in some instances as being tall and masculine-looking and having short hair. In this study less than 10 percent of the men but more than 65 percent of the women wrote stories high in fear of success imagery. The predominant responses for John underscored the realization of the man's ideal and enhancement of his self-image by success. Heightened levels of aspiration often followed this initial success. Horner also found that women who seemed to be high in fear of success worked best in achievement settings in which there was no interpersonal competition and in which achievement was noncompetitive. Thus these women performed more efficiently in a nonaggressive solo situation.

Superego structure may demand that aggression be turned on the self rather than outwardly directed, even in an appropriate assertive manner. If the superego is especially critical of self-assertion, equating it unconsciously with aggression, the result may be self-effacing or masochistic characteristics.

Unresolved dependency needs hiding behind a veneer of autonomy and self-sufficiency may propel a career-oriented woman toward success, entailing the denial and repression of these needs. Once the woman has achieved success, the dependency needs are intensified, along with the defenses against them. At this point the facade of self-sufficiency must intensify into toughness, harshness, and aggressiveness, with avoidance of closeness and intimacy, further enhancing the woman's unhappiness.

On the other hand, a woman may attempt to preserve a homeostasis in her marriage or family by impeding success in the larger world. If competition with the husband is intolerable, if the woman cannot tolerate separation from her child, or if her dependency on her husband serves in subtle ways to preserve equilibrium and stability in the relationship, these factors will serve as a regressive pull, around which rationalizations are built. At times this equilibrium is preserved in minuscule ways, such as the wife asking her husband something about which she knows and can decide for herself.

At times the choices are handled by *either* being career woman *or* wife and mother. To marry and bear children, and to be loved, is the woman's "calling" in the latter instance. The vertical split between the self that is wife and mother and the self that is successful in a career exists when there is difficulty in integrating the two. Some women labor with the perception of themselves as successful imposters in this regard.

The cultural factors which have been stressed in numerous studies highlight some women's fear of departing significantly from the culturally reinforced model of the female, including binding qualities of passivity and dependency. The negative consequences expected from success include social rejection, as well as a fear of being unfeminine. Although these cultural aspects are real, they do not speak to the complexity of the underlying and deeply rooted fear of success that some women have. Furthermore, it is currently a more prevalent cultural ego ideal for a woman to succeed; some even believe that it is imperative for a woman to succeed in order to live up to this ego ideal.

Lillian Rubin (11) interviewed 160 women. The average age of the respondents was 42.5 years. They averaged ten years spent entirely in the roles of wife, mother, and homemaker. There were many answers to her question "Give me an idea of who you think you are." Consistent, however, were answers including being a mother and a wife. Marriage and motherhood were the tasks by which most women felt they were judged, validated, and identified.

One of the women Rubin interviewed, who was a highly successful executive, described herself initially as a "good cook." This disavowal of success, power, and assertion epitomizes one of the conscious manifestations of a dichotomized perception of oneself.

Women who are changing their world and horizons are at times not able to change their view of themselves. To be competent and to feel competent may be different. Acknowledging competency to themselves and others is often an avoided recognition. The woman may fear stepping out of bounds of what is considered feminine. The achieving woman may violate social and internal expectations which rattle stereotypic expectations. Ambivalent about the old self and the new, a woman may vacillate between old ideals and newly found competency. There is a fear of being seen as too strident, aggressive, and unfeminine.

CHAPTER 11

———

Work Compulsion in Women

WORK COMPULSION is closely related to work inhibition but manifests as its opposite. The work addict ("workaholic") is incessantly driven, relentlessly active. Inactivity or any activity other than work engenders guilt or anxiety about inadequacy and self-worth. The compulsion to work is a defense through action against such underlying concerns as inadequacy, guilt, invalidation, and worthlessness.

Like the mythical Sisyphus, who endlessly pushed a huge rock to the top of a hill, only to have it roll down again, the person with work compulsion cannot rest. Working passionately, long, and hard, and experiencing satisfaction from work, do not mean work addiction. It is only when the person *cannot do without work* to maintain comfort or a sense of worth that she is addicted.

In a psychoanalytic study of work compulsion, Kramer (1) describes its underlying patterns, including feeling like an imposter, struggles related to authority figures, the need for recognition and fame, and a continuing sense of inadequacy.

Work can become a means to withdraw from relationships, manipulate relationships by limiting one's availability, or moderate relationships which are overstimulating sexually or aggressively. The wish for admiration is a profound underpinning for many work compulsions. Immersion in work may be a compulsive attempt to reverse feelings of diminished self-esteem. Enslaved by the drive to prove herself powerful and adequate, the individual constantly turns her attention and energy to new sources of attainment, acquisition, and relentless striving. Although seeming to attain what is most sought, the compulsive worker is still dissatisfied.

If admiring confirmation and approval by parents in response to the child's achievements were not part of her experience, one outcome may be an intense, driven ambition to get response and admiration from as many sources and in the greatest quantities possible. This unrelenting ambition, the driven need for approval and validation, is the basis for some work compulsions. Even remarkable successes are not permanently gratifying. Each accomplishment may be met, upon completion, with a letdown or even depression, as if the goal were the pursuit of challenge rather than an accomplishment itself. When the goal is completed, excitement diminishes quickly. The echoes of the applause die when emptiness begins to be experienced, and a new source of external admiration through accomplishment is sought.

For the individual with narcissistic pathology, work may become a central organizer, a means to self-validation. One woman with profound pathological narcissism—who could, however, function at a very high level at her job—described the meaning of work to her. "My work reassures me. When I feel overwhelmed, I turn to my work, which I know well, and I feel calmed. I became an achiever because it's something I could do that would exist in time and space and become objectively real. It gives me pats on the back." She further described how she used work for continuity and stability, and when there was any disruption in her life, she became even more immersed in work to reestablish internal order. She didn't remember her parents ever holding her or calming her. When she became upset as a child, she would retreat to her room to furiously engage in (what was to her, then) work.

Very few of these individuals may be seen in treatment, however, as they are often considered successful by themselves and others, and receive substantial gain from their achievement—as long as accomplishment is on an ascending scale. When a goal is reached, it is often experienced as a kind of deprivation: love can no longer be earned by performing well. So reaching a desired goal is not actually satisfying. Reaching a goal, much like leisure time or vacations, adds to the feeling of unworthiness, nonproductivity, and guilt. The personal tragedy of a successful, hardworking, and aggressive person of this type is the relentless demand to escape from the perception of guilt or inadequacy. There must always be a challenge and a conquest. The re-creation of the basic scenario perpetuates itself, unless examined therapeutically, throughout life. Although the names of the characters change, the same psyche is writing the script with its recurrent themes.

One woman was described by her friends in the following way (2):

> She is so ambitious that one cannot help but think it is over-compensatory. I can't imagine her relaxed and trusting anyone. She is remarkably neat, proud, well-groomed, efficient, dependable and service-oriented. Sometimes in her enthusiasm and self-confidence, she does not realize that she has offended or used others. . . . She is a person who tries to excel in everything she undertakes. As a person who never experienced failure or difficulty, she is not very sympathetic toward other students and at times is inconsiderate of them. She is obsessed with the idea of personal success and has spent her entire life obtaining it.

Success based on perfectionistic striving, relentless personal demands, and feared loss of love can provide external reward but at disproportionate internal cost. Achievement based on this type of motivation is usually precarious because this motivation is not intrinsically sustaining, but rather a hope for a certain kind of external validation. This motivation is also conflictual and compromised, and the resultant comfort, happiness, and esteem are ultimately unsatisfactory. A case report will illustrate some of these psychological issues.

CASE STUDY: THE FASTER DANCER

Beth had just been offered a position as coordinator of a major division of her corporation, a significant advancement in the accelerated career of this thirty-three-year-old woman. Nevertheless, she felt that she was inadequate and a failure as a wife because accepting this position would preclude accompanying her husband to his new job in another city. Although his promotion was of much less magnitude than hers, she felt distraught, torn between following him and accepting a major career advancement.

A frenzy of work intensified her already accelerated style. She often worked twelve to sixteen hours a day, feeling anxious and uncomfortable unless she was doing something she identified as productive. Weekends were as difficult as other leisure periods, when she felt the urge to be active and productive, and guilty if she was not.

Work had been characterized by an unrelenting stream of accomplishments, each seeming only to increase her diligence in pleasing and being applauded by her superiors. The milieu of all her accomplishments seemed to contain a sense that she was not appreciated or recognized sufficiently, thereby clouding the setting with her veiled anger. Her response was to work harder; the driven quality of her work disallowed relaxation, pleasure, or even enjoyment of accomplishment. There was an almost palpable fear that when a project was completed the "love" gleaned from performing well would come to an abrupt end.

Her aggression could not be revealed to others without supreme guilt—work had become the only vehicle. Her guilt had made her feel inadequate, as her superego constantly berated her for her hostility. No matter how much she achieved, however, she could not satisfy her demanding superego.

As a child, she had received little overt warmth and love from her parents. She made adamant efforts to obtain affection by her accomplishments—by becoming more "perfect," striving to please harder and harder.

Her father was very demanding, yet constricted the range of his daughter's interests to well-accepted pursuits for women; for example, he extolled the virtues of a career as a secretary. Although she was told she had brilliant promise as a dancer, her father would not allow her to participate in training that was funded by a highly coveted national scholarship. The mother then took a job to provide for her transportation to a summer retreat to pursue her scholarship without her father's permission. Upon completing her rigorous and dedicated training, she performed for her father. After a flawless, gifted rendition of a lengthy and difficult ballet, she turned to her father in expectation of praise and support. The father's only remark was, "Don't you know any ballroom steps?'' She was first hurt, then angry, and only in treatment recognized the intensity of her rage toward this perfectionistic yet withholding father, for whom she danced faster and faster, awaiting the applause that was never forthcoming.

She ultimately saw the father in a more objective light, recognizing how he managed his own sense of inadequacy and anger by projecting them onto his daughter, criticizing her rather than himself.

She had carried a lifelong burden of regarding herself as bad and flawed. If she allowed herself to become close to any man, she reasoned unconsciously, he would then see how she "really was." She had had a number of unsatisfactory and broken relationships, including two marriages, each of which had common threads running throughout. The most evident thread was a joyous "honeymoon" period in the beginning of the relationship filled with idealism and hope. This feeling inevitably gave way to the discovery of a "fatal flaw" in every man: he seemed to undergo a metamorphosis into a critical and insensitive, self-serving person who had his own and not her best interests at heart.

How this happened with each relationship was somewhat complex, but two elements were central. One precursory element was the unconscious selection of the kind of person with whom she had a relationship. One of her major determining criteria was the need for someone who was unable to engage in a close, mutual, open relationship. Some men were married, some had a limited amount of time in town, but all seemed to disparage and to conquer women. Each relationship ended in hurt, a feeling of being rejected, and a vow to never get involved with another man.

Beth began one therapy session by wishing she were in a pair of jeans, which would be more comfortable, rather than the dress she was wearing, since she had to "act like a lady" in it. The "lady" whom she had to act like, she realized, was her mother, who was passive, demure, and long-suffering—qualities synonymous with proper femininity. Her father wore the pants in her family and the family revolved around him. She then wished that the therapist would "go to bat for her" and tell her husband how worthwhile she was and how much better she was doing since her treatment began. She suggested a joint session in which she, her husband, and the therapist would meet together. She would act, she proposed, as a cheerleader as the therapist would vigorously and aggressively tell her husband these things. She portrayed how assertive she would be in cheering the therapist on from behind. The therapist noted her assumption that she was without a bat and could not go to bat for herself, but could only assert herself in displaying support. The anger and frustration engendered by that restraint were explored. She stated, "I realize that it's different to hate a man than it is to hate the color brown or green beans. To hate a man is to hate a part of yourself that you project onto the man. To hate a man is to hate the lack of power, surety, and strength that you see in yourself. You hate what you are when you are with a man."

Difficulties with her self-concept and self-esteem were sequelae of the particular kind of emotional interaction she had with her mother. When Beth was a young girl, her mother was energetic and interactive with her *until* the father came home. Then all focus centered on him. Her mother was not able to remain supportive and invested in Beth's interests and needs because she felt unable to say no to the father, who demanded the focus of attention. She and Beth both believed that to oppose the father was to enrage him—a debacle to be avoided at all cost. In attempting to explain her experiences to herself, Beth concluded that it was she who was not good enough or adequate enough to elicit the kind of responses from both her mother and father that she wanted and needed. A continued escalation of striving to be "good" expanded to trying to be perfect, since being just extremely good was not sufficient. Attempts to be perfect did not elicit the responses she wanted either, so a chronic sense of inadequacy and a basic depressive mood resulted. Assertiveness was inhibited and she retreated emotionally. Another response was to "dance faster": to attempt to be more pleasing, perfect, and hardworking. If she stopped her compulsive work, she was likely to recognize how angry she was and how driven the "dancing" was.

The wish for the therapist both to reflect a sense of goodness inside her and help her integrate her partly grandiose and partly devalued self was fused into the issue of what kind of woman she was. She tried to be the best patient, to perform outstandingly in therapy as she had elsewhere. Her fantasy of having the therapist meet with her and her husband was laced with Oedipal elements, including the fantasy of being the only woman in the room, for whom both her husband and the therapist would be vying. Tongue-in-cheek, she stated that she was certain that she was the therapist's only patient, and that he had nothing to do all week but wait for her appointment each Thursday. The grandiose and Oedipal competitive issues in this "only child" are interwoven.

The re-creations with subsequent men of her earliest relationship with a man (her father) were designed to right the traumatic wrong that was experienced with her father. Each person was selected because he embodied certain characteristics: older, handsome, intense, absorbed in a career, hardworking, bright, and unavailable emotionally. The attempt was to wrest from fate a different outcome; this time, she hoped, her "father" would be caring and loving, and whatever happened when he turned cold and critical would be understandable and not her fault.

The second major element was then activated. The deposit of the hurt, the devasting unpredictability of her father's anger and criticism, was inside her in the form of anger toward men. Finding the anger unacceptable, she projected it onto a man, experiencing it as coming from him. The anger became real and not just a transference perception, assured by her choice of men and by her exquisite manipulations to discover and excite their anger.

The ensuing drama had a particular purpose. In addition to hoping for a better solution this time around than with the father, she hoped to convert a passive experience into an active one by fighting back and/or leaving. This attempt to master a previously traumatic situation was doomed to failure because the original conflict was unconscious. Endless repetitions left her with the inevitable frustration of repeated, aborted relationships and the validation that "all men are the same." These repetitions did not detoxify her conflict and/or correct her self-perception, because their essence was unconscious. Each of the men had played his part rather than wonder why the script was written for him in a particular way—an insight available in psychotherapy or psychoanalysis that is rarely discovered elsewhere.

SECTION IV

———————◆———————

Treatment of Women with Success Phobia

CHAPTER 12

———◆———

Specific Treatment Issues

THE POTENTIAL of psychoanalytically oriented therapy is to make more of an individual available for satisfying, creative, and adaptive experiences. The process of psychotherapy or psychoanalysis may allow one to be in touch with parts of oneself which have been neglected, forgotten, omitted, or pushed away—yet which continue to exert major influence currently (1).

As treatment unfolds, one learns of the fantasies and assumptions that influence one's destiny. One may be imprisoned by these fantasies and assumptions. Many of these may be unconscious, while others may be the continuation of a social and cultural context which may contain constricting values, myths, and conformity. During treatment old conflicts become alive; neglected parts of the self are reawakened. Self-investigation allows a freedom to mourn the past, to invest oneself wholly and fully in the present. "What was" and "what might have been" can be replaced with "what is" and "what can be." If this does not occur, one may, as in the words of a popular song, "lose tomorrow looking back for yesterday."

155

Psychological events are private, and access to one's own being is limited internally by unconscious censoring devices; in addition, an elaborate conscious censoring device limits access by others. This privileged access, coupled with unconscious repression, disallows full understanding of the motivational aspects of behavior for most people outside a treatment situation. By understanding behavior and intent in a new way, through insight, one can not only redefine perceptions of oneself and others, but be more fully aware of the underlying and unconscious attitudes and beliefs that govern the definition of self and pursuit of personal life goals.

Emotion and behavior are personal creations. The creation of an unhappy event or affect in one's life in which one sees oneself as a victim can also be seen as a personal creation in an attempt at mastery. Thus one may *re-create* penalties or impediments to successes. Emotional perceptions are re-created using the template of unconscious and infantile logic, which serves as the original matrix of the emotions.

The perception of an actual event becomes the emotional creation of the child, as it is interpreted and represented to the child in a unique manner in her own mind. This is dramatically validated by therapy patients when they collaborate with a sibling on a mutually shared and remembered event, finding that they have strikingly different perceptions of the same event. Two siblings often have two very different perceptions of the same parent, even of the basic personality of the parent. This can be illustrated by discussion between two adult brothers about their childhoods. One brother described his relationship to a father who was cold, obsessive, distant, and authoritarian. The other brother was quite surprised, remembering the father as warm, spontaneous, supportive. They, of course, were *both right*—they were describing their own experiences, perceptions, and memories of the father, which constituted their *psychic reality*.

Treatment is a "corrective developmental experience," the freeing up of developmental fixations and conflicts. It is also an experience of further development and structural change in the context of a complex relationship with another human being, the therapist. Developmental learning involves a major affective experience in integration—not just expressive exposure and factual examination, as in scholastic learning—and it takes time.

Women, as well as men, seek psychiatric and psychological help because they are in pain. A thorough descriptive and dynamic assessment aims to understand the patient and illness as thoroughly as possible, to make a scientific prescription for a specific type of psychotherapy, and to formulate a treatment plan within the mode of therapy chosen (2).

An understanding of internal organization and motivation is necessary to an understanding of behavior. A behavior may be only the manifest aspect of variant, diverse, and complexly multidetermined issues. For example, to say that someone stops just short of completion of major tasks, or that she sabotages success, is an observation of phenomenological data conceptualized at the level of repetitive patterns of behavior. The question then has to be asked: "Why?" That is, the underlying aspects of motivation must be addressed. Development is an adaptive process, and the understanding of developmental issues must consider the context within which it has occurred. Stereotypic expectations or impositions of unbending theory prevent the full blossoming of mental process and content in the treatment situation. Scientific thought and theory which help to organize clinical data should illuminate rather than control understanding of the patient's material.

Therapy and Therapists' Biases

Therapists and patients may accept cultural stereotypes as standards. A therapist may allow a belief that women should marry and have children to unwittingly shape interpretive posture and influence the outcome of treatment. Likewise, the therapist may assume that a man should get along with his career and establish a family as a part of mature development. Professionals may have different concepts of mental health for female and male patients (3). Many culturally accepted viewpoints may find themselves infused into treatment, including stereotypes of women as passive and dependent or beliefs that these traits are not consistent with optimum mental health. Since the objectives of psychotherapy or psychoanalysis involve not merely the relief of pain but the understanding of oneself and the resolution, hopefully definitive, of underlying issues creating symptomatology, these issues are vital to facilitate optimum growth. Therapy, ideally, will provide a woman the opportunity to acknowledge and overcome the barriers which impede her full utilization of her own potential.

To perceive as internal all of the important and problematic issues facing women is as fallacious as interpreting them exclusively in a social context. Psychoanalytic theory has been among the last intellectual disciplines to reflect a non-male-oriented view of personality and development; society in general gives little recognition to unconscious forces. Mitchell (4) argues that a rejection of psychoanalysis would be fatal for feminism, because psychoanalysis "is not a recommendation *for* a patriarchal society, but an analysis *of* one." Lerner states: "The failure of therapists to analyze sufficiently the defensive and maladaptive determinants underlying a patient's choice to conform to culturally prescribed notions of femininity is a common phenomenon in psychotherapy" (5). Another limitation which can exist is the failure of a male therapist to recognize an unconscious need to please him and remain unthreatening. A woman may become a "good patient" and sacrifice her growth and autonomy (5).

In therapy, we must differentiate as much as possible between factors originating within the woman and factors originating within society. Constraints and directives based on earlier perceptions and an earlier (though still current) internal model must be made. In doing this, new data impinge on an old, comfortable model, and the result may initially be discomfort. A woman may, on the other hand, fear losing her motivation and drive to succeed, especially if she senses that they emanate from conflict. Similarly, the artist may fear losing her creativity and motivation should the conflict driving and fashioning them be resolved. Resolution of internal struggle does not destroy motivation or creativity, but frees the individual for even greater realization of her potential as well as enjoyment of the fruits of her achievements.

Increased awareness, and changes in expectations and possibilities, have brought to many women possibilities for alternative life patterns and identifications. Conflicts may arise between consciously, rationally sought goals and orientations and expectations derived from early life experiences. Traditional psychotherapists and psychoanalysts, however, tend to focus *exclu-*

sively on intrapsychic conflict without considering the cultural matrix which has been both adapted to and incorporated. Through this adaptation and incorporation, this matrix becomes a component of current perception; it has helped fashion the internal representation of the world and of the individual self within it. Our internal representation of the *world*, just as our internal representation of our *self*, determines to a major degree our perceptions, experiences, and choices seen as available. Each individual creates a model, based on individual experiences, and this model becomes a private and individual reality—an individual's unique point of view. If this model includes socially agreed upon fictions such as stereotypic sex role constraints, this, too, is internalized. For the adult woman, then, changes in society and in external constraints are not enough: she must also address what is now an internal constraint based on her developmental experience. The external constraint has become an internal constraint for her.

Even though the objective world may contain multiple alternatives and choices, the model of the world and of the woman's self exists as if an earlier context were still present. This model has not allowed a recognition of and shift to a current context—a different way of thinking about oneself and the world. Each individual and each model must be evaluated and understood in the person's own domain. Constraint to one point of view, one conceptual level, or even one theoretical point of view may obfuscate important material.

Empathy as a Listening Perspective

The full appreciation of a patient's internal world is prerequisite to helping the patient recognize, objectify, understand, and resolve compromise-producing (symptomatic) progeny. We do not, in our science or any other, discover absolute truths, but seek frames of reference which make possible wider understanding, prediction, and explanations in the simplest way possible free of internal contradiction (6). A frame of reference which has particular therapeutic relevance is the nature and clinical use of empathy.

Empathy is a particular listening perspective. The vantage point is the internal experience of the patient. Listening is done from the inside of the patient, so to speak, rather than as an observer. Both therapist and patient then come to focus on the patient's subjective reality (7). Barbara Tuchman speaks to this principle most cogently in her book *In Search of History*: "If the historian will submit himself to his material instead of trying to impose himself on his material, then the material will ultimately speak to him and supply the answers."

Empathy does not mean being overtly comforting, supportive, sympathetic, or commiserative. As a listening perspective, it allows the therapist to appreciate another frame of reference—the patient's. The focus is on the inner experience of the patient, including emotions, perceptions, ways of thinking, and causal explanations: the individual's entire experience. Empathy allows a comprehension of a patient's feelings and thoughts using ourselves as therapists—in resonance with the patient's internal experience. In so doing, the vantage point changes from that of an external observer or a particular theory to one of comprehending the inner experience of another (8). Empathy becomes a bridge of understanding between human beings with widely different frames of reference: the echo in one of the voice in another.

The therapist's ability to empathically understand and communicate this understanding is essential to the patient's free expression of her own reactions and internal experiences, which is in turn a prerequisite to introspection, understanding, insight, and change. This partial identification with another—surveying the scenery from that viewing point within the other person—is not an end in itself, but aims to foster understanding. Empathic understanding is a precondition to working through and grieving past identifications and constrictions.

The Sex of the Therapist

The "fit" of patient and therapist is important, but often gets overemphasized, as there are neurotic and unconscious factors in the choice of a therapist or analyst, an inability of the patient to know the person and training of the therapist objectively, and a referral network which does not consider many variables that may be based on highly subjective criteria. A major determinant is the quality of the therapist. Training as well as experience are major determinants of a therapist's ability to work effectively with the patient.

The question may arise as to the appropriate sex of a therapist or analyst for a woman. The search for an identification model remains an important aspect of therapist choice for some women. While it is possible that women may be conscious of their wish to identify with a female therapist or analyst as a prototype of a successful professional woman, there may also be an unconscious hope of borrowing magical powers. A woman therapist or analyst may be paradoxically devalued in the woman's mind by appearing less formidable than a man. In seeing a male therapist, a woman may have to deal with the trepidation of coming into direct experience with fantasies and conflicts about a man. Her concern may be about failure of empathy and understanding by a male who she fears might react as a *man* rather than a therapist. A concomitant concern is that a male therapist might impose values in a subtle way or be unable to accept the vantage point of the woman and her femininity. In some cases, these concerns are well founded.

The trend of women seeking women physicians and therapists may reflect another facet: an increased self-esteem in women, such that they may no longer themselves depreciate other women. Approximately two-thirds of patients in therapy and analysis are women and 89 percent of psychiatrists are men (89 percent of the 24,000 members of the American Psychiatric Association). Symonds (9) states: "While women are experiencing themselves as needing and wanting to grow beyond the role of traditional dependency and are trying to overcome their excessive need for others to take care of them, many men react to this by feeling rejected and misunderstood. Paradoxically, men also feel victimized; they are often hurt or angry over being unappreciated."

In an optimal treatment with a sensitive and knowledgeable professional capable of empathic, nonbiased work, *all* the important issues will emerge and be scrutinized. The gender of the analyst or therapist may determine the *order of appearance* of the various issues (e.g., with an opposite-sexed therapist Oedipal issues may come to focus more rapidly, while with a same-sexed therapist pre-Oedipal issues may first emerge), but ultimately the important issues will be resolved regardless of the chronology of their emergence.

Empathic failures on the part of the therapist do occur, even though the therapist may have been analyzed in order to prevent blind spots in therapeutic work. As they occur, the failure and the resulting affect in the patient can be discussed, as well as interpretation of the underlying wish. For example: A patient in analysis briefly mentioned as she began a session that she had been looking for a copy of a certain periodical (*The Wilson Quarterly*), which she needed for an upcoming presentation. Her thoughts seemingly carried her away from this topic, and I thought no further of it. As the hour progressed, I became aware of a growing sense of aloofness, isolation, and anger in the patient. When I observed that she had somehow gotten quite distant and her associations indicated a kind of preoccupation, she stated that she was extremely angry with me. She said that I must have known that I had this periodical in my waiting room and that she wanted to borrow it. She felt I was trying to make it difficult for her. I reflected that I had been unaware of her inner response until she mentioned it. I then interpreted her wish that somehow I would know what she was thinking without her putting it into words—as if we were two bodies with one mind. What ensured was a most productive examination of her wishes to be understood by me, her parents, and others—and a growing recognition that many of the current "empathic failures" she experienced from others were orchestrated by the remnants of the omnipotent infantile wish to be the central focus of a maternal person who can sense a need or wish without it being spoken. With this awareness, she could recognize, for example, how sensitive she was to those empathic failures, constituting an insight into an exquisite type of sensitivity which she had experienced most of her life. By this process she gained an understanding of her dependence on the external affirming function of others and the important role this played in her own self-esteem; she had concluded with each failure that she must be unlovable and worthless or she would have been understood and responded to.

The role that a patient plays in orchestrating empathic failures needs to be examined when it occurs. A transferential assumption that a therapist will not understand becomes enacted by not expressing thoughts, feelings, experiences, or perceptions which in fact insure that the therapist does indeed not understand. The patient's expectation becomes a reality, validating her assumption that the therapist, as all other (people) (men) (women) (adults) in her life, does not fully understand her. Interpretive work must be done so that the patient can recognize what a vital and initiating role she plays in this re-creation of her past and perpetuation of her expectation.

This is another potential area where internal conflictual and transference issues may hitchhike on male–female stereotypes and dichotomies. The propensity for a patient is to transferentially view her therapist at particular times in treatment as a superego projection: punitive, critical, and authoritarian. This expectable phase in treatment occurs even with a sensitive, empathic, and knowledgeable therapist. Reports abound, however, of innumerable examples of insensitivity complicating this aspect of treatment, and the *accurate perception* of a therapist whose values or resistance to the new roles is contrary to the awareness for which women are striving must be distinguished from the *transference perception* of the therapist as being like a figure from the past.

Ticho (10) indicates that in analysis with a male analyst a revised self-image will be no more difficult to achieve than with a female analyst. She even adds: "During the course of analysis with a male analyst there will be plenty of opportunities for the female patient to find in her life situation such models for mature female identifications. This material will come up in the analysis and can be analyzed just as well in the transference neurosis with the male analyst." She adds, however, that "difficulties may arise with a male analyst who has problems in accepting his feminine identification." Lerner, however, indicates that "in intimate dyadic relationships, men have very little experience relating to women in a truly equalitarian manner"(5).

It is essential that therapists be aware of their own biases and values in order to fully understand patients without contaminating the relationship with their own personal values or conflicts. Predetermined ideas of what type of woman or person a patient is supposed to be are anathema to facilitating recognition and complete understanding of the *individual*.

The issues of maternal and paternal transference have an inherent facet of bias. Transference phenomena represent the re-creation and reexperience of attitudes, feelings, and behaviors toward someone currently in the patient's life (notably the therapist or analyst) that were directed toward an important figure, usually a parent, in the past. The transference phenomena are rooted in the perception of parents as they behaved toward the patient throughout development. For a therapist to imply that a nurturing, empathic, and deeply caring set of feelings is "maternal" transference is to imply that this is not or could not be a part of the way the child experienced the father. This attribution of certain qualities, as derived from the perception of the mother or of the father, may be analogous to the bias which characterizes certain qualities as inherently feminine or masculine. Similarly, strong assertive feelings and attitudes may not necessarily be "paternal" transference.

A patient's view may also be seen as a transference distortion of a current situation based on expectations, attitudes, or ideas from the distant past, rather than being considered as an issue of differing systems of values. Alternatively, in many instances a differing set of values may be a resistance vehicle to propel the patient away from perplexing and painful internal issues. Nowhere in therapy is a basic assumption and value system more relevant than in the treatment of women, particularly in regard to the issues described in the preceding discussions. The question of values, on the part of both the therapist and the patient, has to be kept in mind. From the therapist's point of view, this scrutiny must be personal, and the patient not burdened, since the focus of treatment should be the patient and her internal experience and perception. Reality versus transference, transference and countertransference, and the basic set of values from which an interpretive posture is fashioned should be carefully scrutinized by the therapist in order to sensitively and empathically appreciate the patient's view of herself and her world through *her* eyes. Listening from within the patient is most possible when approached in this manner. The therapist may have an unspoken and heretofore unquestioned assumption that "getting well" for the patient would be, for example, to resolve the conflicts which prevent her from wanting children or from entering marriage. Middle-class standards which may seem a natural part of life for certain therapists may be the template against which normality is measured, rather than the therapist recognizing those values which uniquely belong to each patient.

A "personal myth" exists for each individual: the conscious memories of autobiographical data are the memories of the perception of events, feelings, and reasoning. A perception of reality is full of omissions, distortions, and personal elaboration. It is nevertheless the individual's reality, because it is his or her set of experiences as well as an evolving self-definition. The individual's personal myth extends from past history to the present. One's self-perception as well as aspects of one's way of life, successes and failures, may be regarded as repetitions of the fantasies of the personal myth. As an example, one woman had developed, as a girl, the feeling that she was very ugly—particularly that her skin was very ugly, not the right color, and that her moles made her skin untouchable. She was surprised to learn in treatment that this long-held belief had formed basically because her mother never touched her in a caressing or soothing manner. She simply concluded that she was "untouchable" and that it must be for some reason: most concretely, because she had ugly and horrible skin.

In viewing emotion, constraint, perception, and other psychological functioning as an active process that is created moment by moment, the therapist can help the patient discover the active, here-and-now nature of an impediment, and the patient's role in fashioning it. Interpretations can then be made about how, for example, in experiencing her parents as wanting her to fit into a certain mold, *in agreeing with those voices from the past,* she feels restrained at the *present moment* by *actively creating* the same mold. Action language in therapy, as first elaborated by Schafer (11), can be a particularly useful way to talk about issues seen previously in a passive way, using passive language.

The origins of the inhibition of the patient's potential, and the degree of her ego integration and strength, including both developmental and descriptive diagnosis, must be assessed as part of the overall picture of the person. For those patients who have both the need and the ability to undergo analytically oriented psychotherapy or psychoanalysis, the possibility exists of a definitive resolution to inner conflict. How and why that which was once adaptive is now no longer adaptive must be recognized and mourned.

The liberation of women, like the liberation of men, is an internal as well as an external issue. It is a freedom to act and be one's self, freedom from inner and outer constriction and stereo-typic constraint, freedom from exclusion and mistreatment, and freedom from fear and confusion. Internally, it is a freedom from maladaptive defenses caused by dominating anxiety, from rebel-liousness, from unhealthy or blocked competitiveness, and from anger or vindictiveness, as well as from self-contempt. History cannot be changed, but one can be freed from its constraint.

References

Chapter 1
Biological and Social Variables:
A Review and Reappraisal

1. SHERFY, M. The evolution and nature of female sexuality in relation to psychoanalytic theory. *J. Amer. Psychoanal. Assoc.* 14: 28–128, 1966.

2. BELL, R. Relations between behavior manifestations in the human neonate. *Child Develop.* 31: 463–477, 1960.

3. LIPSITT, L., and LEVY, N. Electrotactual threshold in the human neonate. *Child Develop.* 30: 547–554, 1959.

4. LEWIS, M. Studies of attention in the human infant. *Merrill-Palmer Quart.* 11: 95–127, 1965.

5. SHERMAN, J. *On the Psychology of Women.* Springfield, Ill.: Thomas, 1971.

6. MONEY. J. *Love and Love Sickness: The Science of Sex, Gender Difference, and Pair-Bonding.* Baltimore: Johns Hopkins University Press, 1980.

7. SALZMAN, L. Psychology of the female: a new look. *Arch. Gen. Psych.* 17: 195–203, 1967.

8. MURPHY, L., and MORIARITY, A. *Vulnerability, Coping and Growth.* New Haven: Yale University Press, 1976.

9. BLOCK, J. Personality development in males and females: the influence of differential socialization. Paper presented at annual meeting of the American Psychological Association, New York, Sept. 1979.

10. MOSS, H. Sex, age, and state as determinants of mother-infant interaction. *Merrill-Palmer Quart.* 13: 19–36, 1967.

11. GOLDBERG, S., and LEWIS, M. Play behavior in the year-old infant: early sex differences. *Child Devel.* 40: 21–31, 1969.

12. THOMAS, E., and GAULIN-KREMER, E. Correlates of human parental behavior: a review. In J. Money and H. Masaspha (eds.), *Handbook of Sexology.* New York: Excerpta Medica, 1977.

13. YARROW, L. *Infant and Environment: Early Cognitive and Motivational Development.* New York: Halstead Press, 1975.

14. ROSENFIELD, E. The relationship of sex-typed toys to the development of competency and sex-role identification in children. Paper presented at the meeting of the Society for Research in Child Development, Denver, 1975.

15. FEIN, G.; JOHNSON, D.; KOSSON, N.; STORK, L.; and WASSERMAN, L. Sex stereotypes and preferences in the toy choices of twenty-month-old boys and girls. *Develop. Psychol.* 11: 527–528, 1975.

16. WHITING, B., and EDWARDS, C. A cross-cultural analysis of sex differences in the behavior of children aged three through eleven. In S. Chess and A. Thomas (eds.), *Annual Progress in Child Development.* New York: Brunner/Mazel, 1975.

17. CHODOROW, N. Family structure and feminine personality. In M. Rosaldo and L. Lampere (eds.), *Women's Culture in Society.* Stanford, Ca.: Stanford University Press, 1974.

18. MACCOBY, E. *Social Development: Psychological Growth in the Parent-Child Relationship.* New York: Harcourt Brace Jovanovich, 1980.

19. PIAGET, J. Piaget's theory. In P. Mussen (ed.), *Carmichael's Manual of Child Psychology.* New York: John Wiley & Sons, 1970.

20. TERMAN, L., and ODEN, M. *Genetic Studies of Genius,* vol. 5. Stanford, Ca.: Stanford University Press, 1959.

21. RUMBAUT, R. Personal communication, 1982.

22. EPSTEIN, C. Bringing women in: rewards, punishments, and the structure of achievement. In R. Kundsin (ed.), *Woman and Success:*

The Anatomy of Achievement. New York: William Morrow & Co., 1974.

23. SHAINESS, N. The working wife and mother—a "new woman"? *Amer. J. Psychother.* 34: 374–386, 1980.

24. GREENACRE, P. Women as artists. In *Emotional Growth.* New York: International Universities Press, 1971.

25. EPSTEIN, C. Women's attitudes toward other women—myths and consequences. *Amer. J. Psychother.* 34: 322–333, 1980.

26. DINNERSTEIN, D. *The Mermaid and Minotaur.* New York: Harper & Row, 1977.

27. MILLER, J. (ed.). *Psychoanalysis and Women.* New York: Brunner/Mazel, 1973.

Chapter 2
The Concept of Gender

1. BLUM, H. Masochism, the ego ideal, and the psychology of women. *J. Amer. Psychoanal. Assoc.* 24: 157–192, 1976.

2. MONEY. J., and EHRHARDT, A. *Man and Woman, Boy and Girl.* Baltimore: Johns Hopkins University Press, 1972.

3. STOLLER, R. *Sex and Gender.* New York: Science House, 1968.

4. _____. Etiological factors in female transsexualism: a first approximation. *Arch. Sex. Behav.* 2: 47–64, 1972.

5. _____. Primary femininity. *J. Amer. Psychoanal. Assoc.* 24: 59–78, 1976.

6. MONEY, J.; HAMPSON, J. G.; and HAMPSON, J. L. Imprinting and the establishment of gender role. *Arch. Neur. Psychiat.* 77: 333–336, 1957.

7. LESTER, E. On the psychosexual development of the female child. *J. Amer. Acad. Psychoanal.* 4: 515–527, 1976.

Chapter 3
Separation–Individuation Issues

1. MAHLER, M. On the significance of a normal separation-individuation phase. In M. Schur (ed.), *Drives, Affects, Behavior,* vol. 2. New York: International Universities Press, 1965.

2. HALPERN, H. Psychodynamic and cultural determinants of work inhibition in children and adolescents. *Psychoanal. Rev.* 51: 173–189, 1964.

3. STOLLOROW, R. Reflection on self psychology. Seminar. Boston: Boston Psychoanalytic Society, 1980.

4. GALENSON, E. Examination anxiety in women. Unpublished paper, 1982.

5. MAHLER, M.; PINE, F.; and BERGMAN, A. *The Psychological Birth of the Human Infant: Symbiosis and Individuation.* New York: Basic Books, 1975.

6. KINSLEY, D. The developmental etiology of borderline and narcissistic disorders. *Bull. Menninger Clinic* 44: 127–134, 1980.

7. MASTERSON, J., and RINSLEY, D. The borderline syndrome: the role of the mother in the genesis and psychic structure of the borderline personality. *Int. J. Psychoanal.* 56: 163–177, 1975.

Chapter 4
Narcissism: Healthy and Pathological

1. KOHUT, H. *The Restoration of the Self.* New York: International Universities Press, 1977.

2. _____. A note on female sexuality. In P. Ornstein (ed.), *The Search for the Self.* New York: International Universities Press, 1978.

3. STOLLOROW, R. Toward a functional definition of narcissism. *Int. J. Psychoanal.* 56: 179–185, 1975.

4. BERGER, M., and KENNEDY, H. Pseudo-backwardness in children: maternal attitudes as an etiological factor. *Psychoanal. Study Child* 30: 279–307, 1975.

5. HALPERN, H. Psychodynamic and cultural determinants of work inhibition in children and adolescents. *Psychoanal. Rev.* 51: 173–189, 1964.

6. APPLEGARTH, A. Some observations on work inhibitions in women. *J. Amer. Psychoanal. Assoc.* 24: 251–268, 1976.

7. STEELE, B. The psychic development of abused children. Paper presented during Grand Rounds, Baylor College of Medicine, Houston, Texas, 1980.

8. BAKER, H. The conquering hero quits: narcissistic factors in underachievement and failures. *Amer. J. Psychother.* 33: 418–427, 1979.

Chapter 5
Sexual Identity: Formation and Elaboration

1. GREEN, R. The significance of feminine behavior in boys. *J. Child Psychol. Psychiat.* 16: 341–344, 1975.

2. KRUEGER, D. Psychotherapy of adult patient with problems of parent loss in childhood. *Curr. Con. Psychiat.* 4: 2–7, 1978.

3. _____. Childhood parent loss: developmental impact and adult psychopathology. *Amer. J. Psychother.* (to be published).

4. KOHUT, H. A note on female sexuality. In P. Ornstein (ed.), *The Search for the Self.* New York: International Universities Press, 1978.

5. _____. The self in history. In Ornstein, *Search for the Self.*

6. FRANKEL, S., and SHERRICK, J. Observations of the emerging sexual identity of three- and four-year-old children: with emphasis on female sexual identity. *Int. Rev. Psy.* 6: 297–309, 1979.

7. ROIPHE, H., and GALENSON, E. Early genital activity and the castration complex. *PSA Quart.* 41: 334–337, 1972.

8. _____. Object loss and early sexual development. *PSA Quart.* 42: 73–94, 1973.

9. PARENT, H.; POLLOCK, L.; STERN, J.; and KRAMER, S. On the girl's entry into the Oedipus complex. *J. Amer. Psychoanal. Assoc.* 24: 79–108, 1976.

10. ERICKSON, R. Womanhood and the inner space. In J. Stourse (ed.), *Women and Analysis.* New York: Grossman Publishers, 1974.

11. APPLEGARTH, A. Some observations on work inhibitions in women. *J. Amer. Psychoanal. Assoc.* 24: 251–268, 1976.

12. BRUNSWICK, R., and FREUD, S. The pre-Oedipal phase of the libido development. *PSA Quart.* 9: 293–319, 1940.

13. LESTER, E. On the psychosexual development of the female child. *J. Amer. Acad. Psychoanal.* 4: 515–527, 1976.

14. EDGECUMBE, R. Some comments on the concept of the negative Oedipal phase in girls. *Psychoanal. Study Child* 31: 35–62, 1976.

Chapter 6
Oedipal Issues: The Taboo of Success

1. ERIKSON, E. *Childhood and Society,* 2nd ed., pp. 255–256. New York: W. W. Norton & Co., 1963.

2. Blum, H. Masochism, the ego ideal, and the psychology of women. *J. Amer. Psychoanal. Assoc.* 24: 157–192, 1976.

3. Shapiro, T., and Perry, R. Latency revisited: the age seven plus or minus one. *Psychoanal. Study Child* 31: 79–105, 1976.

Chapter 7
Adolescence: The Emerging Self

1. Adelson, J., and Douvan, E. *The Adolescent Experience*, pp. 347–348. New York: John Wiley & Sons, 1966.

2. Blos, P. *On Adolescence: A Psychoanalytic Interpretation.* New York: The Free Press, 1962.

3. Ketsdevries, M. Defective adaptations work: an approach to conceptualization. *Bull. Menninger Clinic* 42: 35–50, 1978.

Chapter 8
The Development of Work Identity and Self-Esteem

1. Erikson, E. *Identity and The Life Cycle.* New York: International Universities Press, 1959.

2. Marcus, I. The influence of development upon career achievement. In S. Greenspan and G. Pollock (eds.), *The Course of Life: Psychoanalytic Contributions Toward Understanding Personality Development.* Vol. 2: *Latency, Adolescence, and Youth.* Washington, D.C.: National Institute of Mental Health, 1980.

3. Adelson, J., and Douvan, E. *The Adolescent Experience.* New York: John Wiley & Sons, 1974.

4. Hennig, M. Family dynamics and the successful woman executive. In R. Kundsin (ed.), *Women and Success: The Anatomy of Achievement.* New York: William Morrow & Co., 1974.

5. Lozoff, M. Fathers and autonomy in women. In Kundsin, *Women and Success.*

6. Clance, P., and Imes, S. The imposter phenomenon in high-achieving women: dynamics in therapeutic intervention. *Psychotherapy: Theory, Research and Practice* 15: 241–247, 1978.

7. Moulton, R. Women with double lives. *Contemp. Psychoanal.* 13: 64–84, 1977.

8. DeRosis, H. *Women and Anxiety.* New York: Delacorte, 1979.

9. Symonds, A. Neurotic dependency in successful women. *J. Amer. Acad. Psychoanal.* 4: 95–103, 1976.

Chapter 9
The Psychology of Work

1. Erikson, E. *Insight and Responsibility.* New York: W. W. Norton & Co., 1964.

2. Piaget, J. *The Moral Judgment of the Child.* New York: Harcourt, 1932.

3. White, R. *Psychological Issues.* Vol. 3, no. 3, monograph 11: *Ego and Reality in Psychoanalytic Theory.* New York: International Universities Press, 1963.

4. Murphy, L. *The Widening World of Childhood,* New York: Basic Books, 1962.

5. Sarnoff, C. *Latency.* New York: Jason Aronson, 1976.

6. Cotton, N. Childhood analogues to the adult capacity to work. Paper presented at American Psychiatric Association meeting, May 1980, San Francisco.

7. Nadelson, C., and Notman, M. Child psychiatry perspectives: women, work, and children. *J. Amer. Acad. Child Psychiat.* 20: 863–875, 1981.

8. Halpern, H. Psychodynamic and cultural determinants of work inhibition in children and adolescents. *Psychoanal. Rev.* 51: 173–189, 1964.

9. Low, I. Family attitudes and relationships: a summary. In R. Kundsin (ed.), *Women and Success: The Anatomy of Achievement.* New York: William Morrow & Co., 1974.

10. Scott, J. Early childhood influences. In Kundsin, *Women and Success.*

11. Padan, D. *Intergenerational Mobility of Women: A Two-Step Process of Status Mobility in a Context of Value Conflict.* Tel Aviv University, Israel, 1965.

12. Lozoff, M. Fathers and autonomy in women. In Kundsin, *Women and Success.*

13. Symonds, A. Phobias after marriage: women's declaration of dependence. *Amer. J. Psychoanal.* 31: 144–151, 1971.

14. BINGER, C. Emotional disturbances among college women. In G. Baline (ed.), *Emotional Problems of the Student*. New York: Doubleday & Co., 1961.

15. ERIKSON, E. Womanhood and the inner space. In J. Stourse (ed.), *Women and Analysis*. New York: Grossman Publishers, 1974.

16. RAPOPORT, R., and RAPOPORT, R. N. *Dual Career Families*. London, England: Penguin Books, 1971.

Chapter 10
Success Inhibition

1. FREUD, S. Some character types met with in psychoanalytic work (1915). In *Collected Papers*, New York: Basic Books, 1959.

2. WALLACE. L. Thoughts on the business of life. *Forbes*, Nov. 24, 1980.

3. APPLEGARTH, A. Some aspects of female psychology related to achievement. Unpublished paper, 1976.

4. MAHLER, M. Notes on the development of the basic moods: the depressive affect. In Loewenstein et al. (eds.), *Psychoanalysis—A General Psychology*. New York: International Universities Press, 1969.

5. SCHECTER, D. Fear of success in women: a psychodynamic reconstruction. *J. Amer. Acad. Psychoanal.* 7: 33–43, 1979.

6. MURPHY, L. *The Widening World of Childhood*. New York: Basic Books, 1962.

7. OVESEY, L. The phobic reaction: a psychodynamic basis for classification and treatment. In E. Goldman, (ed.), *Developments in Psychoanalysis*. New York: Columbia University Press, 1966.

8. KRUEGER, D. Anxiety as it relates to "success phobia": developmental considerations. In W. Fann, I. Karacan, A. Pokorny, and R. Williams (eds.), *Phenomenology and Treatment of Anxiety*. New York: Spectrum Publications, 1979.

9. JOREEN. Trashing: the dark side of sisterhood. *Ms.* magazine, April 1976.

10. HORNER, M. Femininity and successful achievement—a basic inconsistency. In J. Bardwidk, E. Douvan, M. Horner, and D. Gutmann (eds.), *Feminine Personality and Conflict*. Belmont, Ca.: Brooks-Cole Co., 1970.

11. RUBIN, L. *Women of a Certain Age: The Midlife Search for Self*. New York: Harper & Row, 1979.

Chapter 11
Work Compulsion in Women

1. KRAMER, Y. Work compulsion—a psychoanalytic study. *Psychoanal. Quart.* 46: 361–385, 1977.

2. LELAND, C., and LOZOFF, M. In *College Influences on the Role of Development of Female Undergraduates.* Educational document ED-026975. Bethesda, Md.: ERIC, 1969.

Chapter 12
Specific Treatment Issues

1. POLLOCK, G. On aging and psychopathology. *Int. J. Psychoanal.* 63: 275–282, 1982.

2. KRUEGER, D. Clinical consideration in the prescription of group, brief, long-term and couples psychotherapy. *Psych. Quart.* 51: 92–105, 1979.

3. BROVERMAN, I.; BROVERMAN, D.; CLARKSON, F.; ROSENKRANTZ, T.; and VOGEL, S. Self-role stereotypes and clinical judgments of mental health. *J. Consul. Clin. Psychol.* 39: 1–7, 1970.

4. MITCHELL, J. *Psychoanalysis and Feminism.* New York: Pantheon Books, 1974.

5. LERNER, H. Special issues for women in psychotherapy. In M. Notman and C. Nadelson (eds.), *The Woman Patient.* New York: Plenum Publishing, 1982.

6. PETERFREUND, E. On information and systems models for psychoanalysis. *Int. Rev. Psychoanal.* 7: 327–345, 1980.

7. SCHWABER, E. Empathy: a mode of analytic listening. *Psychoanal. Inq.* 1: 357–392, 1981.

8. ORNSTEIN, P. Remarks on the central position of empathy in psychoanalysis. *Bull. Assn. Psychoanal. Med.* 18: 95–108, 1979.

9. SYMONDS, A. Men psychiatrists and women patients. *Frontiers of Psychiatry*, Feb. 1, 1980, p. 14.

10. TICHO, G. Female autonomy and young adult women, *J. Amer. Psychoanal. Assoc.* 24: 139–156, 1976.

11. SCHAFER, R. *A New Language for Psychoanalysis.* New Haven: Yale University Press, 1976.

Index